In episodes that cover almost seventy-five years of hockey history, well-known hockey authority Stan Fischler describes the amazing antics of such greats as King Clancy, Frank Boucher, Red Dutton, Gump Worsley, Lester Patrick, and Emile Francis. He tells about the night that a goose named Mildred ruffled the dignity of the top executives of both the American and National hockey leagues; the players who "borrowed" a trolly for a joyride back to their hotel; "Perfect Pierre," the imaginary goalie who was taken seriously by Boston Bruin fans. The author also describes the comeback of Larry Zeidel, an elderly defenseman who used Madison Avenue hard-sell techniques to promote himself; and he tells the strange tale of "Leone's Magic Elixir," a vile black liquid that helped to stimulate an amazing winning streak for the New York Rangers.

These and many other weird, improbable, and hilarious stories present a fascinating behind-the-scenes look at a rough-and-tumble sport and the men who play it.

STRANGE BUT TRUE HOCKEY STORIES

BY STAN FISCHLER

TEMPO
BOOKS

GROSSET & DUNLAP
A National General Company
Publishers   *New York*

CONTENTS

INTRODUCTION

One evening, after a rather zany game between the New York Rangers and the Detroit Red Wings, a reporter asked Ranger manager Emile Francis to explain the illogic of the contest he had just seen.

Francis mulled the question over and then replied, "Hockey is a slippery game—it's played on ice!"

That, in a nutshell, explains the often baffling but never boring behavior of hockey players, their fans, and the men who run the world's fastest team sport. Of course, there have been more involved explanations of the mania that is hockey. Psychologists point out that the long Canadian winter tends to produce a repressed state of mind in pro hockey players, nearly all of whom are Canadian born. They also note that many of the players are of conservative English-Scottish descent. Supposedly the combination of the Canadian cold and the moderation of their ancestors inspires the players to seek an outlet for their aggression. And what better outlet than the slippery ice where mayhem is legalized?

Inevitably the kaleidoscopic capers of the arena bubble over to hotel rooms, railroad trains, trolley cars and other less icy surroundings—which might help the reader to understand why a player named Charlie Conacher once dangled a teammate headfirst out a hotel room window.

Nonpsychological types are less analytical in their appraisal of hockey. Their approach is that any game in which the players dart around and collide with one another at speeds of up to 30 miles per hour, shooting a hard rubber puck at more than 115 miles per hour, is apt to produce a form of zaniness not common to other sports.

It is the kind of game in which an irate team owner named Eddie Shore once locked a referee, Red Storey, in the officials' dressing room after Storey had called an especially harsh contest against Shore's Springfield team. It is also the kind of game that produces the highest decibel counts among fans and the lowest boiling point among players.

"You don't have to be crazy to be in this sport," ex-Ranger manager Frank Boucher once said, "but it certainly doesn't hurt."

I hope that the following strange but true stories will give the reader a better understanding of the often bizarre and always fascinating world of hockey.

Stan Fischler
New York City
June 1970

1. THE BIRTH OF PRO HOCKEY

The origin of the game of hockey has been attributed to many sources. Some authorities claim that the game was the brainstorm of British soldiers stationed in the Canadian cities of Halifax and Kingston in 1853. Others credit students at McGill University in Montreal for initiating the sport. But most hockey historians agree that Montreal gentleman, R.F. Smith, drew up the first rules for the game in the late 1870s. Wherever the game originated, by 1879 there were frequent and enthusiastic matches in Montreal.

Although hockey might have been born in Canada, that country should not receive all the credit for hockey's development in North America. The game was also being played in the United States in such cities as St. Paul, Minnesota; Baltimore, Maryland; and New York City near the turn of the century, and professional hockey was played in the United States before it was in Canada.

Actually, the roots of the National Hockey League can

be traced to the copper-mining area of Northern Michigan, specifically the town of Houghton, which boasted a population of a little more than 3,000. It was there during the 1903–04 season that it all began. A dentist by the name of Dr. J.L. Gibson decided to spend his nondrilling hours organizing a hockey team. Dr. Gibson, himself a Canadian, gathered together a number of Canadians living in the Houghton community and dubbed his team the Portage Lakes.

The Portage Lakes septet—it was a seven-man game in those days—played amateur teams from towns like St. Paul, Minnesota; Sault Ste. Marie, Ontario; and Sault Ste. Marie, Michigan. The newly formed Houghton team, manned by Canadian players, romped through its twenty-six-game schedule, thoroughly enraging citizens in rival towns. In order to provide better competition for Portage Lakes, the other towns began to import Canadian players and pay them handsomely for their services. By the following season (1904–05), there were several professionally staffed teams and the International Professional League was formed.

Contrary to popular opinion, some of the finest hockey players in the world played on the Portage Lakes team for the tiny town of Houghton. In fact, the 1905–06 edition of the team could have passed for an early-day all-star team. The lineup included such early notables as goaltender Riley Hern, point Grindy Forrester, cover point Barney Holden, rover Fred "Cyclone" Taylor, center Bruce "Hod" Stuart, right wing "Bad" Joe Hall, and left wing Fred Lake. Actually, Hod Stuart and Cyclone Taylor were good enough to gain a niche in the Hockey Hall of Fame after its creation in 1940.

In 1907 the United States-born International League gave way to a Canadian edition—the Trolley League of Southwestern Ontario. This was followed in 1910 by the National Hockey Association. Finally the National Hockey League was born in 1917. By that time the town of Houghton was forgotten.

Although New York didn't achieve recognition as a "hockey town" until 1925, when the New York Americans entered the NHL, historians have evidence of hockey being played there in the early 1890s. The game really got organized in 1896 when Bartow S. Weeks of the New York Athletic Club developed the Amateur Hockey League and became its first president.

New York boasted two rinks. One was located in the then independent City of Brooklyn on Clermont Avenue near Myrtle Avenue in the Clinton Hill section, a posh bluestocking community. Dubbed the Clermont Avenue Rink, it housed two teams—the Crescent Athletic Club and the Brooklyn Skating Club.

The St. Nicholas Rink was located in Manhattan, at Sixty-sixth Street and Columbus Avenue. In later years it became the St. Nicholas Boxing Club, but before the turn of the century two hockey clubs were housed there—the New York Athletic Club and the St. Nicholas Skating Club.

To stimulate enthusiasm for the new Amateur Hockey League, the New York Athletic Club's *Journal* published an enthusiastic description of hockey prior to the 1896–97 season:

The game is practically scientific "shinney" on ice skates and is vastly popular with our cousins across the border. It will be found interesting to the most exacting critic, his attention being fully occupied through every moment of play.

From the time the referee blows his whistle signifying the start, the spectators' nerves are kept at a tension not relaxed until the call of time, there being very little or nothing of the element of "time calls," which have proved such fruitful cause of criticism in football.

A player insisting on continually being offside will be sent from the ice, causing a momentary stoppage. Otherwise the time is employed in brilliant rushes, quick checking and clever passing.

Equipment was minimal in those first years of organized hockey, although the wooden sticks bore a striking similarity to those used today. Shoulder and elbow pads were unknown and the skaters wore golf knickers and long stockings. Goaltenders protected their legs with cricket pads, not unlike the goalie pads worn now.

The game itself differed from modern hockey in many respects. There were seven players on a team and all seven men were expected to play the entire game. Substitutions were granted only in the case of serious injury. The referee was the sole judge of the seriousness of an injury. Instead of three twenty-minute periods, the game was divided into two twenty-minute halves and, in case of a tie, one ten-minute overtime period. If the contest was still deadlocked after the overtime, the game was rescheduled.

New York City's first official league game, on December 15, 1896, was at the St. Nicholas Rink in Manhattan. E. A. Crowninshield, a rusher, scored the first goal after three minutes of play on passes from players Tom Barron and R. D. Wrenn. The final score was St. Nicks 15, Brooklyn 0.

The Bobby Hull of the league turned out to be the mustachioed F.S. Wonham of the New York Athletic Club, who scored seven goals as his club routed the Brooklyn Crescents, 20–0, in the opener for both teams. It quickly became obvious that the St. Nicholas Club and the New York Athletic Club were the class of the league. In the final and decisive match between the two powerful clubs, the New York Athletic Club came out on top, 3–1, to become the first hockey champion of New York City.

In later years the New York Rangers and Americans developed an intracity rivalry that matched in intensity that of baseball's Giants and Dodgers before they moved to the West Coast. But they might never have had the opportunity to cash in on the rich hockey market that had developed if it had not been for the St. Nicholas Skating Club and the New York Athletic Club, the teams that helped nurture the game in its early, vital years.

2. THE ODYSSEY OF THE STANLEY CUP

Hockey's most revered possession is the Stanley Cup, emblematic of the world's championship and, along with tennis' Davis Cup, one of the two most cherished trophies in the world of sports. Curiously, though, the Stanley Cup wasn't originally meant to be awarded to the champions of professional hockey. It was intended to be presented to the leading amateurs of Canada.

Even more ironic, the man after whom it was named—Lord Stanley of Preston, Canada's governor-general—really didn't give a damn about hockey. His son, Arthur Stanley, was the hockey buff in the family and he, along with his aide, Lord Kilcoursie, and Ottawa publisher P. D. Ross, persuaded Lord Stanley to purchase the silver mug in 1893 and award it to the leading amateur team. The cup, valued then at $48.67, was first won by the Montreal Amateur Athletic Association. It remained in the amateur ranks until 1912, when it was captured by a professional team, the Quebec Bulldogs.

6

If Sir Arthur Conan Doyle had spent his writing years in Canada, there's every reason to believe he'd have penned a few adventures of Sherlock Holmes and the Stanley Cup. One of the earliest and best cup stories occurred in 1905 after the Ottawa Silver Seven had won the cup.

Jubilant Ottawa fans had presented their champs with a gala victory dinner that sent many of the victors well into the grape. Finally the party ended and the Ottawa skaters stumbled home in the bitter cold of the night. As refreshing as the Arctic air may have been, it wasn't enough to clear the mind of Harry Smith, a stalwart of the Silver Seven. Through Harry's somewhat distorted eyes, the revered cup took on all the aspects of a football. He grabbed the trophy and delivered a perfect place-kick that sent the Stanley Cup arching into the Rideau Canal.

Since the other troops were no more sober than Smith, the cup remained in the Rideau and the Silver Seven headed home. The next morning, Harry Smith began to suspect that he had been guilty of a rather rash place-kick. He dressed quickly, dashed back to the Rideau Canal, and there he found the cup, nestled in the bone-dry bed.

The dents that Harry's boot had put in the cup weren't to be its last. A year later, the Montreal Wanderers captured the championship and proudly, and somewhat more soberly, hauled the cup to the studio of a photographer named Jimmy Rice. There they proudly lined up for the traditional victory portrait with the Stanley Cup standing before the victorious Wanderers.

When Jimmy Rice gave the final click of the shutter, the Wanderers gleefully filed out of the studio for the nearest pub. Perhaps the visions of malt hops were dancing in their heads. Whatever it was, the Wanderers jubilantly departed and never gave a thought to the trophy.

In fact, nobody but a charwoman was concerned about the cup. When the last of the Wanderers had left the studio, the cleaning lady noticed the interesting silver cup sitting on the floor. "My," she must have said, "but this would make a lovely flower pot." So she took the Stanley Cup home.

Several months later, the Wanderers' management thought it would be a noble gesture if the Stanley Cup were placed on display in the victors' arena. But, alas, where was the trophy? The last place anyone remembered seeing it was at Jimmy Rice's studio. Jimmy was contacted. He called his charwoman, who explained that the Stanley Cup was on her mantel—literally in full bloom.

In 1924, when the Montreal Canadiens captured the cup, they were feted by the University of Montreal in a public reception at the National Monument in Montreal. After the reception, the Canadiens were invited by the team's owner, Leo Dandurand, to a party at his home. Before they got there, the cup managed to escape again. According to Dandurand, here's how it happened:

"Georges Vezina, Sprague Cleghorn, Sylvio Mantha, and I got into a Model T Ford to make the trip. The little lizzie stalled going up Cote St. Antoine Road in Westmount and we all got out to push. Cleghorn, who had been jealously carrying the cup in his lap, deposited it on the curb at the roadside before he joined us in shoving the car up the hill. When we reached the top, we hopped back into the car and resumed our hockey chatter as we got going again.

"Upon reaching my house, we all started in on a big bowl of punch my wife had prepared. It wasn't until she asked, 'Well, where is the Stanley Cup you've been talking about?' that we realized Cleghorn had left it on the side of the road. Sprague and I drove hurriedly back to the spot almost an hour after we had pushed the car up the hill. There was the cup, in all its shining majesty, still sitting on the curb of the busy street."

As the cup grew older, it grew proportionately in size. In order to inscribe the names of each new winner on the trophy, it became necessary to enlarge the base of the cup again and again until it more than quadrupled its original size. And as the trophy grew, greater and greater security measures were taken to protect it from thieves and players with short memories. Even so the cup managed to get away.

During the play-offs of April, 1962, the cup resided in a huge glass case right in the midst of the Chicago Stadium lobby for all to see. The Black Hawks had won the world championship the previous year and were now engaged in another furious battle for the trophy.

A Montreal fan by the name of Ken Kilander took a dim view of the Stanley Cup's residing in Chicago. He studied the silver mug and the glass case with the intensity of a safecracker about to launch a great heist. The temptation proved too much for him, so he did it. He opened the glass case and when, to his supreme amazement, neither gongs nor sirens nor any form of warning buzzer sounded, he gingerly reached in and plucked the cup off its stand.

9

Still not a sound. There was just one thing to do. Leave. And that he did. Nursing the cup with affection, Kilander sauntered through the lobby of Chicago Stadium and headed for the exit doors. It was almost too good to be true.

Kilander was just a few yards from freedom when a cop spotted him and asked why he happened to be carrying the Stanley Cup out of Chicago Stadium.

Kilander's retort will never win him entrance into Bartlett's *Familiar Quotations,* abridged or unabridged, but it might get him a prize for sincerity. "I want to take it back where it belongs," he explained. "To Montreal."

Being a Chicagoan, the cop disagreed. He returned the cup to the glass case where it belonged, and Kilander was urged to permit cup movements to be decided on the ice.

3. STRANGE TALES
FROM YESTERYEAR

With a few exceptions, the Stanley Cup play-offs have been held regularly since Lord Stanley of Preston donated the prized trophy. Nature often intervened to impair the quality of the ice in the 1890s and early 1900s before the advent of artificial ice rinks.

Death intervened in 1919 when a continent-wide epidemic of the black flu infected some of the Montreal Canadiens, who were playing the Seattle Metropolitans in Washington. The series was canceled after five games had been played—each team had won two games and one had ended in a draw—and "Bad" Joe Hall of the Montrealers had died of the disease.

It has long been thought that only death or nature has caused an interruption or cancellation of the series, but on one occasion neither was responsible. In 1899 the Montreal Victorias and the Winnipeg Victorias were to meet for the championship. Montreal was the defending champion as the series opened in Montreal. The home team captured the opening game and the second match was tied, 3–3, when the series suddenly disintegrated.

The beginning of the end came soon after the Winnipeg ace, Tony Gingras, was whacked across the knees by a member of the Montreal club. Gingras was so badly wounded that he was hardly able to pull himself across the ice to the Winnipeg bench.

In those primitive days of ice hockey, it was customary for players to go through an entire game without subsitution. However, if a player was so badly injured that he could not continue, the referee had the option of allowing an alternate to replace the disabled skater.

Naturally, the Winnipeggers requested a substitute, but the Montrealers argued that Gingras was not really hurt that badly. The argument raged back and forth, with referee Jack Findlay in the middle of it taking abuse from both sides. Apparently Findlay was a lot less thick-skinned than today's arbiters, because he skated away from the disputants, climbed over the boards, and walked to the dressing room, where he removed his skates, put on his shoes, and left the arena.

By the time the opposing players had simmered down, they realized that they had lost a referee in the process and hastily agreed that Findlay must be found. A Montreal official ordered a horse and sleigh and, with whip in hand, sped to the referee's house. There, to his dismay, he discovered the disgusted arbiter already in bed. Using the most diplomatic phrases at his command, the Montreal official persuaded Findlay that it was all a mistake, that he was loved and respected by all parties, and that his return would be welcomed by both teams. The romancing finally got through to the referee, who piled out of bed, dressed, and returned to the rink on the fast-moving one-horse-open sleigh.

Upon his arrival at the rink, Findlay headed for the referees' dressing room and went about the business of getting ready for the match. He put on his sweater, began lacing his skates, and was all for resuming the game, except for one thing.

The referees' room was situated directly between the Montreal and Winnipeg dressing rooms, separated from them by tissue-thin walls. As a result, Findlay was able to hear distinctly the conversations in both locker areas. He listened with growing fury as players from both teams chastised him in no uncertain terms as a referee of the lowest caliber.

That did it! Findlay stormed out, shouting that he had had it with these ingrates and was going home. Before any more honeyed words could be offered him, he disappeared again into the cold night, vowing never to return. Without a referee, there could be no finals. So the series was canceled and the Winnipeggers took the next train west, all because of a hypersensitive referee.

Verbal attacks weren't the only form of abuse absorbed by the pioneer officials. Plenty of physical harm was inflicted on them, especially before the birth of the face-off. In the early days a hockey match was started in a very complicated manner. First the referee would place the puck on the ice at the approximate center of the rink. Then he would take in his hand the blades of two opposing players' sticks and place them against the puck, at which point, theoretically, he'd step back and shout, *"Play!"*

However, this early version of the face-off worked in theory only. Often an opposing centerman, fearful of losing the draw, would anticipate the referee's call and try to nudge the puck closer to him. Naturally, the enemy center would retaliate, and before the referee could step aside, he inevitably received a solid thwack in the ankles.

This demoralizing, if not painful, situation existed for years until a perceptive referee named Fred C. Waghorne came up with the solution. It seems that Waghorne had been clouted several times during one game and decided enough was enough. So he called the two opposing centermen aside and said he had a new plan. The players would line up as usual, except that their sticks would remain about a foot apart. Waghorne would remain out of harm's way but still close enough to drop the puck between them. Once the puck hit the ice the players could scramble for it. The idea appealed to both sides and worked superbly for the remainder of the contest. Before very long Waghorne's brainstorm was adopted as standard operating procedure in leagues across Canada, and referees became a healthier and happier lot.

A considerably more expensive and outlandish brainstorm emerged a few years later just after the Klondike gold rush furore had subsided. A number of very rich miners from Dawson City in northwest Canada decided that it was high time the Klondike was represented in the Stanley Cup competition. (Prior to 1917, when the National Hockey Association became the National Hockey League, any team could challenge the current holder of the Stanley Cup. A series of games was arranged and the winning team carried off the cup and held it until another challenger managed to win it.

So the miners assembled a team and challenged the powerful Ottawa Silver Seven to a series in the Canadian capital. It was a bizarre idea from the beginning. For one thing, the Klondike team had to travel more than four thousand miles by the most primitive means of transportation and, for another, they had only one player, Lorne Hanna, who came close to passing for a major leaguer, by even the most remote standards.

Undaunted, the boys from the Northwest invaded Ottawa in January, 1905, and, to the surprise of many, almost made a contest of the first match. They ultimately were defeated, 9–2, but it was enough to kindle hopes that the second match would be even closer, if not a triumph for the Klondike.

But the bubble burst with a deafening bang in the second game. The man responsible for defeating the visitors almost single-handedly was Frank McGee, the husky blond Ottawa center whom many regard as one of the greatest players in hockey history, despite the fact that he played with only one good eye.

It took McGee seven full minutes before he gathered up steam, but once rolling he was unstoppable. One-eyed Frank scored two goals within thirty seconds and proceeded to go on a rampage that nearly mummified the Dawson City goaltender. When it was over McGee had scored fourteen goals, a Stanley Cup record that probably will never be approached, let alone equaled. The final score was Ottawa 23, Dawson City 2.

4. THE VANISHING AMERICANS

The true test of a real old-time hockey fan is whether he can recollect a New York Americans game. For almost every hockey devotee who was a fan during the twenties has a story to tell about that incredible team.

The Americans had as much color as their star-spangled uniforms and their owner, millionaire bootlegger "Big Bill" Dwyer, put together. That's a lot of color. Dwyer was a story in himself. Brought up within rock-throwing distance of the old Madison Square Garden, he became a prominent peddler of illegal alcohol during the zany Prohibition days of the twenties.

The fact that Big Bill served a couple of years in Sing Sing prison didn't seem to matter. Everybody—cops, cronies, customers—thought he was an unusual chap. And the fact is, he was. Big Bill had never heard of ice hockey when sportswriter Bill McBeth told him he ought to buy a team and play it out of New York. But Dwyer wrote a check for $75,000 and bought the entire Hamilton, Ontario, Tigers franchise. Today $75,000 would be the going rate for a good minor-league defenseman.

The year was 1925, and for the following decade it was better than even money that wherever the Americans were, on or off the ice, all hell would be breaking loose. Tall Thomas Patrick "Tommy" Gorman was the first manager of the "Amerks," as they were nicknamed, and a more ideal personality could not have been found for the job. He knew his hockey and he loved a good gag, and there was a surplus of both in the Americans.

As for the hockey, it was abundantly competent, if not sensational. The team consisted of the Green brothers, Shorty and Red, who flanked center Billy Burch, giving the Amerks a line of extraordinary ability; forward "Bullet" Joe Simpson, who had a shot as exciting as Bobby Orr's; and defensemen "Big Leo" Reise (whose son was later to play for the Rangers, Alec Kinnon, and Lionel "Big Train" Conacher, voted Canada's Athlete of the Half Century. As net minder, the Amerks had Roy "Shrimp" Worters, who emerged as one of the better little goaltenders of the time.

In those days money was a piddling matter to the Americans. Even though Dwyer was taking a modest loss on his hockey team, he was raking in so much on his bootlegging business that he couldn't spend it fast enough. What's more, hockey was catching on in New York and the instant success of the Americans inspired Madison Square Garden to go out and form a second New York team, the Rangers.

The Amerks forced tough Newsy Lalonde to quit as coach after the 1926–27 season when the club did not reach the play-offs in its division. Shorty Green took over

17

as bench manager the next year and lasted exactly one season. They finished second in their division, the best they'd ever do, but were eliminated in the first round of the play-offs by the Rangers.

Nevertheless, manager Tommy Gorman decided to take the club on a postseason exhibition trip that eventually brought them to Portland, Oregon, for a game with the local team. By this time, all the players knew that Dwyer, a first-class bootlegger, also had a first-class mob, and it was not unusual for some of his all-star gangsters to show up at hockey games.

Unknown to the Amerks, the Portland management had a unique way of announcing that a period of play had ended. At the end of the first period, a loud gunshot that sounded like a cannon blast went off, and the Americans reacted appropriately. Gorman remembered it well:

"Johnny Sheppard and Tex White fell right off the bench, while Roy Worters and Lionel Conacher raced like a Mutt and Jeff team from the vicinity of our net to the nearest boards and scrambled right over them. A couple of our other players on the ice were so startled that they lost their balance and fell flat on their pants."

Maybe that last fact was symbolic. The Americans finished fifth the next season and eventually Big Bill Dwyer was arrested and convicted as a bootlegger. While Dwyer was in the penitentiary the club's debts began mounting. By the time he got out in 1935, the bills were enormous and Dwyer was broke. The team needed a multimillionaire to bail it out. Fortunately, the father of the Americans' superb defenseman, Mervyn "Red" Dutton, just happened to be a multimillionaire. The senior Mr. Dutton's contracting business in western Canada was doing so well that Red could have played hockey for nothing if he had wanted to. The wealthy Duttons provided the money to keep the team going and continued to do so even after the illustrious Dwyer passed out of the picture the next season.

Red Dutton was right out of the Americans' mold. When he took over as coach in the thirties, he was as vocal as a hungry lion. Once, his Americans were playing in Detroit and Charlie "Rabbit" McVeigh was the linesman. Now, Rabbit and Red were pals from childhood. They had fought together in World War I and played together in the early days of the Amerks. It was Red who had recommended Rabbit as an NHL linesman and it was Red, and perhaps only Red, who knew that Rabbit, as a result of a war disability, was deaf in one ear and was getting a pension from the Canadian government.

In this particular game, Dutton had no sympathy for McVeigh. Too many of the linesman's calls were going against the Americans in what was a bitterly close game. Dutton ranted and raved and tried to get McVeigh's attention whenever play stopped near the Americans' bench, but the Rabbit ignored him.

Finally, when the game ended, Dutton rushed over to McVeigh and startled his old pal with a big smile. Red inquired about his health and told Rabbit he had a friend in the government who could get him a pension increase. McVeigh was touched.

"Aw, Red," he said, "that would be great. But what would you tell the Pension Board about my case?"

Suddenly, Dutton's voice rose about a thousand decibels. "I'll tell them," shouted Red, "you're *blind,* you little squirt."

But the New York hockey fans weren't blind to the growing inadequacies of the Americans. Even though they had developed some outstanding young players like "Bonnie Prince Charlie" Rayner, a goaltender of amazing courage, and "Boxcar" Egan, a defenseman with great color and sock, it was the Rangers, not the Amerks, who were winning Stanley Cups. The Amerks began to grow desperate. They tried to bolster their forces by signing such aging stars as Eddie Shore, but it didn't work. To stimulate attendance, Dutton had the club's name changed to the Brooklyn Americans in the 1941–42 season, but that didn't help either. Even worse, World War II had arrived and the best of the players were leaving for the Canadian armed forces.

The staggering personnel losses and the equally alarming bills were too much for even the redoubtable Red Dutton. The Americans were finally forced to fold in the spring of 1942. But New York's first hockey team will never really be forgotten. For men like Bill Dwyer, Bill McBeth, Shrimp Worters, Lionel Conacher, and Red Dutton are what hockey is all about, and their spirit remains. Bill McBeth and his faith in hockey are particularly remembered each year when the McBeth Trophy is awarded to the outstanding Ranger in the play-offs. The spirit of the Americans abounds whenever stick hits puck and the crowd roars. They were the guys who started New York's undying love affair with hockey.

5. THE ROLLICKING RANGERS

The New York Rangers were admitted to the National Hockey League in 1926 and, almost from the beginning, they earned a reputation for zaniness above and beyond the call of duty. In fact, the first madcap Ranger episode occurred *before* the team actually began its initial season.

Conn Smythe, who later quit the New York organization for the Toronto Maple Leafs, was called upon to organize the Ranger sextet. Since Smythe was a native of Toronto, he ordered that the training camp be held there and designated the Peacock Hotel, on the outskirts of town, as the club's base.

A military-minded man, Smythe ordered a strict curfew for his incoming players and warned them that the hotel door would be locked after midnight. One of the Ranger hopefuls was a defenseman named Ivan "Ching" Johnson. "He came from a part of the country," said *Toronto Globe and Mail* columnist Jim Coleman, "where they didn't even know how to spell the word curfew. Johnson arrived in Toronto with a cargo of luggage that consisted almost entirely of Jersey applejack."

In a matter of minutes, Johnson befriended Frank Boucher, another new Ranger who enjoyed a good gag, and the two left the hotel for a long discussion of the coming season and other such matters as their mutual dislike for curfews. By the time early morning approached, both Boucher and Johnson had decided they should consult with Smythe about his unfair and unwarranted curfew. They hailed a cab and returned to the Peacock Hotel, only to discover that, as Smythe had warned, the door was locked tight.

Undaunted, the pair attempted to climb the hotel fire escape and make their way through an open window, but they lost their footing on the ladder and fell to the ground. Fortunately the applejack went unharmed, so Johnson and Boucher decided there was only one thing to do—return to midtown Toronto.

The pair carried on through the early morning. At about 6:00 A.M., they found themselves at a major intersection where a trolley was about to begin its first run of the morning. The Ranger duo climbed aboard and discovered that the motorman was a jolly old chap, so Johnson and Boucher brought out the applejack and the three of them stood on the trolley guzzling to the tune of "Sweet Adeline."

Finally the motorman realized it was time to begin his trip. But he had his two customers to think of. "Where are you guys goin'?" he asked. Boucher suggested that they would like to head for the King Edward Hotel, where they decided they would stay for the rest of the morning.

The hotel didn't happen to be on the route prescribed

by the Toronto Transportation Commission, but that didn't seem to bother the motorman. He turned off the overhead lights, threw open the control lever, and away they sped. Three blocks later a half-dozen potential passengers stood waiting for the streetcar to stop and pick them up, when to their amazement it roared by like the 20th Century Limited.

Soon the Transportation Commission began receiving irate calls from passengers who insisted that their trolley car had rolled past the stop without so much as decelerating. Fifteen minutes after the motorman began his mad ride, he realized that in order to reach the King Edward Hotel he would have to switch tracks. When the trolley reached the next switch, the motorman stopped the streetcar, walked out with a huge steel crowbar, threw the switch, clambered back aboard, and started the car again. The trolley swerved right at the switch and sped onto the downtown tracks. Five minutes later the three musketeers arrived directly in front of the King Edward Hotel.

Delighted with his gesture, the motorman opened the doors, stepped out like a genuine chauffeur, extended his hand to his guests, and escorted them into the King Edward to finish their applejack. And then it was good-bye to the Rangers for him.

"To this day," said Boucher in retrospect, "we never found out if he got back to the right route or whether he survived that run."

Boucher and Johnson weren't the only jokers on that club. Another was Leo Bourgault, who joined the team after manager Conn Smythe had been replaced by Lester Patrick, "the Silver Fox of hockey," in 1926. Like Smythe, Patrick was a martinet who demanded strict discipline from his charges. He, too, was particularly rigid regarding curfews.

One night the Rangers were in Ottawa for a game with the old Senators. Patrick had warned the players to be back on the team's Pullman by 1:00 A.M.

"We won the game something like 10–1," said Bourgault, now a successful tavern owner in Quebec City, "and decided to celebrate with a party in Hull across the river."

Feeling no pain, the players returned from the party to the Pullman car near dawn. Despite their condition, they were coherent enough to know that they had to tiptoe into the train or there would be trouble. "Don't wake Lester," was the word passed up and down the line, and the "coup" seemingly went well.

The next morning Boucher strolled into the diner, where the implacable Lester was hunched over a dish of bacon and eggs.

"Good morning, Mr. Boucher," said Lester, who always addressed players by their last names when there was trouble. After a few minutes of hemming and hawing by Boucher, Lester offhandedly remarked, "Frank, did you know Butch Keeling walks in his sleep?"

Boucher said no, he didn't. Whereupon Lester explained that Keeling had walked into his compartment at about four in the morning, spilled a quantity of liquid, and murmured, barely above a whisper, "Don't wake Lester!"

Another amusing incident involving Patrick occurred when Cecil Dillon, one of the best old-time Ranger scorers, met with him to negotiate a contract. The veterans had told the rookie Cecil that during the meeting it would be wise to give Lester the impression that he was a year or

24

two younger than he actually was, so he would be able to stay in the league longer. Dillon agreed with the idea. An hour after his meeting with Patrick, Dillon was approached by the other Rangers. "Did you subtract a year?" Boucher asked.

"I certainly did," Dillon replied with fresh confidence. "I told Lester I was born in 1907 instead of 1908."

One of the funniest men connected with the Rangers organization was Tom Lockhart, president of the Amateur Hockey Association of the United States throughout the forties, fifties, and sixties. During the thirties, Lockhart was supervising the amateur hockey games at Madison Square Garden and also was managing the New York Rovers, a first-rate amateur team. He spiced up the Sunday afternoon hockey intermission with ice-skating exhibitions featuring a young Norwegian artist. The petite charmer was Sonja Henie, who went on to become a millionaire star of movies and ice shows.

"Some of my promotions were a little more bizarre," Lockhart recalled. "Once when the Hershey Bears were coming to town I was told about a live bear that could skate. So I thought it would be a good idea to have the animal lead the Bears hockey team on the ice."

Lockhart explained that the bear was outfitted with a pair of skates and handled them well. But his trainer couldn't stand on his blades and it caused an uproar among the crowd.

"As soon as the bear stepped on the ice," Lockhart remembered, "the trainer fell flat on his face. The bear kept skating around pulling the trainer all over the ice."

Rudy Pilous, the last coach to lead the Black Hawks to

a Stanley Cup, in 1961, and a former player for Lockhart's Rovers, was an admirer of Lockhart's promotions.

"One day I was sitting in the penalty box," said Pilous, "and I look up and see three fights going on in the stands. Tom was running over to the box to give it to the referees. All of a sudden, he looks up at the stands and sees all the fights going on. Then he turns to me and says, 'Gee whiz, there's too much action goin' on here for three dollars. I gotta raise the prices.' "

Hall of Famer Bill Chadwick, who played amateur hockey in New York, told how Lockhart persuaded him to become a hockey referee in the late thirties.

"Tom didn't pay much money," said Chadwick. "In fact, I remember handling four games a week and getting fifty-five dollars—and I had to pay all my expenses. It was then I realized that Lockhart was destined to be a great hockey executive."

Often Hockey players will get discouraged about hard times and, when that happens, their playing habits will suffer. The Rangers' habits were suffering so much in the fall of 1950 that in November manager Frank Boucher decided to import a psychologist who he hoped would correct a malfunction in the Rangers' winning habits through hypnotism.

"The doctor had very unusual eyes," said Boucher. "They certainly had a hypnotic quality, a kind of white spot that would compel your attention. Most of the players were quite willing to go along with the doctor's attempt to help us."

Yet the doctor was dismissed after one game, for not only did the Rangers fail to win after the doctor's treatment, but one player refused to have anything to do with him. Nick Mickoski, a gangly and bashful forward, was convinced that Dr. David Tracy was some kind of witch doctor who would do him more harm than good. "When Nick saw the doctor heading for the dressing room," said Boucher, "he ran away full speed and wouldn't return till he left."

6. THE NIGHT THE SILVER FOX PLAYED GOAL

Lester Patrick was one of the most distinguished defensemen ever to grace a professional rink before he retired to become manager of the New York Rangers in 1926. Tall, with white combed-back hair, Patrick was behind the Ranger bench when the Blueshirts went up against the Montreal Maroons in the 1928 Stanley Cup finals.

This was only the second full season of NHL hockey for the New Yorkers, and to reach the cup finals was a remarkable accomplishment. Nobody really expected the Rangers to go all the way and when they lost the first game to the Maroons, 2–0, very few eyebrows were raised.

The second game of the series at Montreal's Forum was a tight defensive battle that featured the superb goaltending of Lorne Chabot in the Ranger nets. A tall French-Canadian, Chabot girded himself at the cage as Nels Stewart of the Maroons bore down on him in the second period.

Stewart, who was to the hockey of the twenties what Bobby Hull and Bobby Orr are to the game today, boomed a shot that took off with surprising velocity. Chabot seemed temporarily mummified by the blast as it sailed straight for his head. Before he could duck, the six-ounce hunk of vulcanized rubber crunched into his head just above the left eye.

Chabot fell backward to the ice and crumpled up into a ball, bleeding profusely. It was obvious at a glance that he would be unable to complete the game. A stretcher was dispatched to the ice and the unconscious Chabot was carried out of the rink and sent to Royal Victoria Hospital.

Still very much in the hockey game, the Rangers' problem now was to find a goaltender. But where?

Lester Patrick dashed around the rink to the Maroons' dressing room and conferred with their coach, Eddie Gerard. Patrick had an idea. "I'd like permission to use Alex Connell of the Ottawa Senators," said Patrick. "He's in the rink and I'm sure he'd play for us."

By contemporary standards "borrowing" a goaltender is a primitive practice, but in hockey's early years it was a customary procedure, if the opposing team agreed to it. In fact, Patrick himself, when he was running the Victoria team, had allowed the Toronto St. Pats to use the very same Eddie Gerard in a play-off series against Victoria. So there was precedent for Gerard to approve Lester's request.

Eddie mulled over the bid for about ten seconds and unequivocally replied, "Hell, no. You can't use Connell!"

Stunned and furious, Patrick stormed out of the room and headed straight for the Ranger players who were huddled in their own quarters. "We don't have a goalie," said Lester, "and Gerard won't let us use Connell. Frankly, gentlemen, I don't know what we're going to do."

The late James Burchard, who covered hockey for the old *New York World-Telegram,* was there at the time. A rollicking sort who thought nothing of swimming across the Hudson River on a dare, Burchard fancied it a stroke of genius when he suggested that Lester don the pads himself. "G'wan, Lester," urged the big, gravel-throated Burchard, "show 'em what you're made of."

Nobody took Burchard's latest brainstorm very seriously. After all, Patrick was forty-five years old and had never been a goaltender by profession. But suddenly he startled the onlookers. "Okay," he muttered, "I'm going to do it."

While some of the Rangers attempted to persuade him that he had no business making a comeback—in goal, no less!—Lester diligently strapped on Chabot's bloodstained pads.

"Okay, gang, let's go," he shouted as he headed for the ramp leading to the ice. A muffled chorus of oohs and ahhs came from the grandstand as Patrick made his way to the net for the traditional practice shots. Realizing the hopelessness of the situation, the Rangers attempted to bolster Lester's hopes as well as their own by pumping some mild shots at his pads. Maybe, they felt, if he stops a few in practice the old boy will think he can stop a few in the game.

The referee signaled the resumption of the game and Patrick rapped his pads in the symbolic goaltending gesture of readiness. Finally the puck was dropped and the Rangers pounced on it. They scarcely let the Maroons touch the disk, and when the Montrealers did manage to get off a shot at Patrick, old Lester turned it away.

Somehow Patrick blanked the Maroons in the second period and when the teams trooped into the dressing room for the ten-minute break the score was still tied, 0–0. All of a sudden the Patrick ploy no longer seemed like a joke. His decision to play goal was a catalyst for the Rangers and they returned to the ice for the third period more determined than ever.

Within fifty seconds Bill Cook had barreled through the Maroons' defense and lifted the puck past goalie Clint Benedict. But the Montrealers weren't about to give up easily. They counterattacked more fiercely than ever, yet the old Silver Fox stood his ground, groaning with every kick-save that strained his aging physique. At last, with only five minutes and forty seconds remaining, Lester cracked. Nels Stewart skirted the Ranger defense, feinted once, and then skimmed the puck past Patrick, making the score 1–1.

Lester held fast after that as the clock ticked its way to the conclusion of regulation time. Then it was sudden-death overtime—the first goal would win. The Maroons were counting on the ancient Lester to fold in the stretch. After all, there was just so much a senior citizen could take.

But somehow Patrick managed to foil the Maroons in the early minutes of the overtime, and soon the momentum —as so often happens in the kaleidoscopic game of hockey—tilted in the Rangers' favor. Frank Boucher, their creative center, captured the puck and made his way up the ice. He zigzagged past a Maroon's defenseman and swerved toward the goal. Benedict crouched in the Montreal goal as Boucher cruised in. The shot was hard and low and the puck flew past the Maroons' net minder. The Rangers had won, 2–1, and Lester Patrick was the triumphant goalie.

To a man, the Rangers clambered over the boards and surrounded Patrick. He was hoisted to their shoulders and carried off the ice in victory. One of the broadest grins of all was worn by Jim Burchard, who patted Lester on the back. Years later, he composed a poem to him:

> 'Twas in the spring of twenty-eight
> A golden Ranger page,
> That Lester got a summons
> To guard the Blueshirt cage.

> Chabot had stopped a fast one,
> A bad break for our lads,
> The Cup at stake—and no one
> To don the Ranger pads.

> "We're cooked," lamented Patrick,
> "This crisis I had feared."
> He leaned upon his newest crutch
> And wept inside his beard.

> Then suddenly he came to life,
> No longer halt or lame.
> "Give me the pads," he bellowed,
> "I used to play this game."

> Then how the Rangers shouted.
> How Patrick was acclaimed.
> Maroons stood sneering, gloating,
> They should have been ashamed.

The final score was two to one.
Old Lester met the test.
The Rangers finally won the Cup,
But Les has since confessed.

"I just spoke up to cheer the boys,
"I must have been delirious.
"But now, in reminiscence,
"I'm glad they took me serious."

James Burchard
November, 1947

7. FROM THE ICE TO THE SUPREME COURT

It's a long way from Madison Square Garden to the New York State Supreme Court, but Myles Lane made the jump with plenty of room to spare. Among the graduates of the National Hockey League—some of whom have traveled from the ice to the Canadian Parliament—Judge Lane ranks as one of the most distinguished. Once you could find him wearing the red, white, and blue of the New York Rangers or the brown and yellow of the Boston Bruins. Now he is in a different garb in a different setting.

He began wearing the black robes on January 1, 1969. Before that he occupied a spacious corner office on the twenty-fifth floor of a towering building in downtown Manhattan in the hush-hush quarters of the New York State Commission of Investigation. There he was part of a team of top-level gangbusters that has probed such mischief as state rock-salt purchase scandals, school construction profiteering, police corruption, and the notorious gangster convention in Apalachin, New York, in 1957.

Prior to becoming a member of the commission, Lane, a husky six-footer with wavy red hair and a soft voice that almost belies his pugnacious face, was a United States attorney who helped send atom spies Ethel and Julius Rosenberg to the electric chair and Alger Hiss to jail. Lane also happens to be the first American ever to play on a Stanley Cup team—the Boston Bruins of 1929.

Lane began his career of "body checking" lawbreakers in 1937, when, three years after graduating from Boston College Law School, he was named an assistant United States attorney for the Southern District of New York, one of the hottest crime areas in the state. He rose to chief assistant in 1950 and became United States attorney for the district the following year.

Hockey had helped Lane become a lawyer. Lane had worked his way through law school by playing the game—first for the Rangers, then for the Bruins—and by managing the Boston Cubs, a Bruin farm team. Today he thinks the game is good training for any prosecutor. "Hockey is rough but there are some aspects of the law that are a lot rougher," he says.

Myles Lane learned how rough both hockey and law could be from first-hand experience. In one of his early games with the Rangers, the rookie forward was dumped on his head by a giant defenseman. Then he remembered hockey's golden rule, taught to him by teammates Ching Johnson and Bill and Bun Cook in training camp: "There are no medals for bravery in hockey. Protect yourself because nobody else will." Lane learned how to play tough, and word got around the league to lay off him.

35

He remembered his teammates' advice years later in the courtroom when an opposing defense attorney needled him and, in effect, tried to put him on trial instead of the defendant. During a recess, Lane tossed one of the prosecution's exhibits in the case to the opposing attorney with obvious annoyance, told the story of his early hockey experiences, and warned that he would ask an extra year in jail for the defendant for every nasty crack. The courtroom quickly quieted down after that.

Lane's pro hockey career had been brief—four years as player and manager—but colorful. He was a competent player, if not a star. And as one of the first Americans in the big league, he had tremendous curiosity value at the box office. This was not always to his advantage, though.

In his first game with the Rangers, his enthusiasm got the better of him. He drew three charging penalties and this comment from Ching Johnson: "Keep this up and you'll be the badman of the league, not me."

In a locker room interview after the game a sportswriter quoted him as saying that "this game is a cinch compared to college hockey." Lane said he was misquoted; what he really meant was that college hockey is physically more tiring because there are fewer substitutions, but that the professionals are far better and more competitive players.

No matter. The damage was done. When the Rangers arrived in Montreal the following Saturday night, the newspapers were exhorting the populace to come out and see the wise guy. "Meet Mr. High Stick," said the headlines, and the arena was packed. The Montreal Maroons were out to get the American college boy who scoffed at the Canadian professionals.

Lane's first rush down ice ended with a bone-crushing

body check and a charging penalty for his overanxious opponent. His next rush ended the same way and so did the third.

Emotions were running high and the game grew rougher. Lane escaped unhurt, but by the time the game was over there were two major casualties. Taffy Abel needed twelve stitches in his foot. And the great Ching Johnson broke his leg, an injury from which he never fully recovered.

Lane thought of Johnson as his big brother and mentor, but as for the greatest player he ever saw, Lane gives the award to Eddie Shore of the Bruins. He was not alone in his admiration. When Lane was with the Rangers, the New York club tried to set up a deal with the Bruins that would have involved trading Myles Lane for Eddie Shore. The Boston reply was quick and to the point: "You're so far from Shore [that is, beneath] you're out of sight."

Within his first year in the league, though, Lane was sold to Boston, where he became Shore's teammate. And, based in Boston, he was more easily able to pursue his law studies. In fact, he chose to work his way through school by playing hockey rather than football or baseball (he was offered contracts in all three sports) because it fit in best with his school schedule. Once Lane got into condition with some rigorous training in the early fall, he needed to practice only one hour a day during the season. He found he could sandwich in a noontime practice session between classes.

During the season one typical week for the hard-charging scholar went something like this: On Tuesday he studied all day, then went to the rink at 7:00 P.M. to play the Rangers; on Thursday he traveled to New York for a return match with the Rangers, back to Boston Friday for classes, and then a train to Montreal for a weekend game. On western trips, to Detroit and Chicago, Lane would either cut classes or, if schoolwork was too heavy, would miss the trip. To keep from getting bored in the fall, and to pick up some more tuition money, Lane coached football, first at Boston University, then at Harvard.

Lane's playing career was interrupted when he broke his back in an automobile accident, but he merely hung up his skates for a while and became manager of the Boston Bruins' farm team, the Cubs. "It was an interesting experience, and a bit sad," he says, "to watch the young players on the way up and the old-timers on the way down."

As for Lane, his professional playing days ended when he got his law degree, but his interest in the game has never lagged. Even now, he is quick to push legal matters to one side of his desk and talk hockey with a visitor.

"Hockey's a lot different these days than when I played it," he says and grabs a long yellow legal pad and desk pen to illustrate. He quickly diagrams a hockey rink and distributes "X's" and "O's" about the ice to represent players. He explains that the most significant rule change in the game was the one that allowed forward passing into any zone. In the old days, only lateral passing was allowed to bring the puck into the defensive zone.

"The result has been a lot less fancy stickhandling than we used to have with people like the Cook brothers and Frankie Boucher," he says. This threesome, incidentally, gets Lane's nomination as the best line ever put together.

"Another result has been less body contact because the defensemen now don't dare risk a body check," Lane says. "On the other hand, there's a lot more speed to the game. Rush and shoot! Rush and shoot!"

Lane would like to see three aspects of the game improved: speed, stickhandling, and body checking. He thinks this could be done with a few rule changes, but he won't reveal what those changes should be. "I'm an American. I don't want to tell the Canadians how to run their game."

The man who went from stickhandler to lawyer grew up in Melrose, Massachusetts. The son of a building contractor, he got his early physical training by working during the summers on his father's construction projects. Myles went to Dartmouth College on an academic scholarship after turning down baseball scholarships to other schools. There he became a baseball, football, and hockey star. In football, he was an all-American back and the nation's leading scorer, with 125 points. "But I had to keep up my grades or lose my scholarship," he said. "I did lose it one semester and had to work hard to get it back."

Lane did his homework, though, and was graduated in 1928. He was offered a scholarship at Boston University Law School, but chose to pay his way through Boston College because of the school's then unique study-and-work program.

After law school, he took a $15-a-week law clerk job, even though he had better offers. "I had to prove to myself I could get by on my legal knowledge, not my athletic reputation," he says.

Apparently he proved he could. In 1937, three years after he was admitted to the bar, he got his appointment as an assistant United States attorney and began prosecuting criminals and Communists. Also, as a special assistant to the attorney general, he handled antitrust suits against the nation's top rubber companies and conducted a tax fraud probe in California.

During World War II, Lane took a leave from the Justice Department to join the Navy. He was an intelligence officer in the Pacific, then returned to Washington to work for Navy Secretary James Forrestal on a special committee to revise court-martial procedures. He left the Navy in 1946 as a commander and returned to the United States attorney's office.

He was first appointed to the State Crime Commission in 1958 by Democratic Governor W. Averell Harriman, and later was reappointed by Republican Governor Nelson A. Rockefeller. Besides his crime-busting job, Lane had a busy private law practice.

"I don't have much time to follow hockey, except in the newspapers," he says. "I don't even do much skating anymore. Used to play squash, but not much time for that either. Do a lot of walking, though."

But it doesn't take much coaxing to get him to talk hockey. "Bill Cook was the best forward I've ever seen," Lane says. "And Howie Morenz was the fastest man for his size. But the best stickhandler was Nels Stewart. He was lethal around the net. You see . . ."

And out come the big legal pad and desk pen.

8. THE PERILS OF KING CLANCY

Pound for pound, Francis "King" Clancy could pass for both the funniest and most accomplished defenseman in National Hockey League history. The King stood about five feet six inches, and weighed in at anywhere from 126 to 140 pounds, depending on the time of the game or the briskness of the match in which he had just played.

But Clancy's small size was never a factor in his decision whether or not to go to battle. He would fight any man, of any size, at any time. And the King is generally believed to have lost more hockey fights than any man who has ever skated in the big leagues, although Chicago Black Hawk center Stan Mikita has a claim on the record, too.

To many observers, Clancy's most famous bout took place in the early thirties against a Montreal Maroon defenseman, Harold Starr. At that time King's Toronto Maple Leafs were the classiest team in the NHL and the

Maroons were regarded as one of the toughest sextets in the business.

Most players instinctively shied away from the big, burly Starr because of his size, not to mention the fact that he was known to have tried his hand at professional wrestling before joining the Maroons. But Clancy treated Starr as if he were only a ninety-eight-pound weakling.

On this particular night at the Maple Leaf Gardens, the Maroons were handing Toronto a healthy pasting and Leaf tempers were becoming more and more edgy. Finally, in the last minute of play, a rather large brawl involving most members of both teams erupted. Normally these mass hockey fights break into two skirmishes. The instigators fight their separate battle and the other players battle mildly or just hold each other until the main event is over. Somehow, more than a few serious individual fights developed this time and, to everyone's amazement, there was Clancy taking on the huge Harold Starr.

The David-and-Goliath-like bout between Clancy and Starr so arrested the attention of the other battlers that they automatically cut short their own fights to see whether the King would come out alive. Some observers had grave doubts about Clancy's ability to survive the clash. For Starr embraced the King with octopuslike arms, dropped the little Leaf to the ice, and then pushed him around the rink as if he was playing broomball with Clancy as the ball. But that wasn't enough. Next he lifted Clancy over his head as a lumberjack would pick up a rock and hurled King about forty feet across the rink. And that still wasn't enough.

Starr skated over to his crumpled foe and concluded the bout by sitting on top of Clancy. Bellowing like a bull moose, Clancy demanded that Starr release him, immediately. And, good sport that he was, the Maroon finally rose to his skates and looked down at the King. As a final insult, Starr said, "That just about took care of you tonight, my friend."

Surrender never came easy to Clancy. He adjusted his disheveled jersey, clambered to his feet, and skated directly to his tormentor. King then delivered what many observers believe is the most significant overstatement ever heard in the NHL. "Starr, you never saw the day you could lay a hand on me!"

Another episode in Clancy's perilous career was reminiscent of a Laurel and Hardy act. It occurred after King had retired to become an NHL referee. He was about to start one game when an obnoxious fan in a rinkside seat began berating him far beyond the limits of even a rooter's discretion. Clancy exhibited remarkable restraint until the spectator trespassed into the realm of King's ancestry. That did it! Clancy dashed to the wooden barrier and clambered over it while the frightened little fan fled up the corridor.

Instead of leaving well enough alone, Clancy continued, galumphing along the rubber matting in pursuit of the spectator. By this time the fan had reached the end of the corridor and disappeared through the exit. Ten seconds later, Clancy, slowed down by the fact that he was wearing a pair of ice skates, also vanished through the mouth of the exit.

A moment later, viewers were greeted by an incredible sight. There, tearing back through the exit at top speed, was our hero, Clancy. Chasing him with fury in their eyes were the little fan and two comrades who appeared to weigh well over 250 pounds each.

Just when they seemed about to lay their ham-sized hands on King's head, Clancy swerved to the right, hopped over the boards, blew his whistle, and dropped the puck for the opening face-off!

Clancy the referee was as competent an official as any other in the league, and he handled games not unlike the way he viewed life in general, with large gobs of humor. And, having been a player, Clancy had good insights into the minds of the skaters he handled during a game. For example, if he missed an infraction that caused a second player to retaliate, it was Clancy's policy to punish the original offender even though King had missed the first play. His instinct told him that there had been a previous offense, and he was usually right.

Occasionally, when players on both teams seemed more inclined to pugilism than puckhandling, he would stand aside and say, "You bums knock yourselves out. I can wait."

One of Clancy's colleagues tells a story about the time the league instituted a program of eye examinations for referees. Apparently King and his court thought that it was a big joke, or, at least, they were going to treat it as one.

When King showed up for his exam, the doctor pointed to the huge letter A at the top of the chart. King squinted as if the A was microscopically small and said he was sorry but he really couldn't see it. Would the doctor mind trying the letters below? An obliging sort, the optometrist pointed at the second line, on which an S and D were quite visibly lined up next to each other. Once again,

Clancy squinted and said he couldn't see them. He then startled the doctor by suggesting that he try the next line, which contained the barely visible letters WERTYU. The doctor consented and Clancy read them off without hesitation. The exam ended there.

Friends of Clancy—and they number in the thousands—often are hard pressed to decide whether King was funnier as a player, referee, or coach. It's probably a toss-up, but those who know King best generally lean toward his playing days. One reason is that Clancy was surrounded by jesters. Teammates such as Clarence "Hap" Day, Charlie Conacher, and Harold Cotton were renowned for their jokes.

During the 1932–33 season, Cotton was victimized by Conacher in one of the most fearsome, and funny, episodes in the annals of the Leafs. It happened after a game in Toronto during which Cotton had had several excellent chances to score. But each time Hal moved into scoring position his linemates somehow overlooked him and failed to deliver the long-awaited pass. This disappointing turn of events happened over and over again until Cotton began to wonder whether there was a conspiracy afoot.

After the game, the Leafs boarded a Pullman heading for New York City and a game the following night against the Rangers. Still furious about being overlooked, Cotton moaned and groaned about his misfortune to just about every player he encountered. The next morning the Leafs checked into New York's Hotel Lincoln (now the Royal Manhattan) on Eighth Avenue and went to their rooms for a pregame nap.

Cotton and Conacher generally roomed together, and on this day they were booked into a room on the twentieth

45

floor overlooking Times Square. Charlie was tired and piled right into bed. Still mulling over his misfortune, Cotton proceeded to stride back and forth in the room berating each of his teammates who had failed to deliver the puck to him.

During the first minutes of the diatribe, Conacher pretended not to hear a word. But when Cotton suddenly announced in a fit of rage that he would obtain retribution by not passing the puck to any of his teammates who were in scoring position, Conacher rose from his pillow and wondered whether he had heard Cotton correctly. Harold wasted no time in repeating his threat.

That did it. Conacher, a man with a physique reminiscent of Paul Bunyan, leaped out of his bed and grabbed Cotton. Charlie knew—as did all the Leafs—that Cotton had an obsessive fear of high places. Out of the corner of his eye Conacher noticed an open window. He carried Cotton to the windowsill, gripped him firmly about the ankles, and literally held Cotton out the open window. Head down, screaming frantically, Cotton could do nothing but stare at the sidewalk twenty floors below.

While all this was going on, Conacher delivered his ultimatum by asking Cotton whether he was or wasn't going to pass the puck. Then, without waiting for an answer, Charlie carefully lowered Cotton another inch toward the street below. Sheer terror brought Harold to his senses and he hurriedly canceled his earlier threats. Whereupon Conacher calmly lifted him up and back into the room. As far as can be determined, it was the last time Cotton ever threatened to be a one-man team.

Another of the legendary Toronto gags involved Conacher, Clancy, and Day, and occurred not long after

Cotton's gripping performance at the Hotel Lincoln. The Leafs had moved on to Boston for a game against the Bruins, and Clancy and Day were rooming together. On such trips, the players usually convened for their pregame meal in the afternoon and then retired to their rooms for a nap.

In those days Bruin games started at 8:30 P.M., so it was customary for Clancy to get up about 6:30 P.M., enabling him to get to the rink about an hour before game time. Conacher and Day huddled shortly after the meal and agreed that it was time for another joke on Clancy.

When King and Hap retired to their room, Clancy set his alarm and soon fell into a deep sleep. Day remained awake and when persuaded that Clancy was well into slumberland, Hap tiptoed out of the room, met Conacher in the hall, and the two of them took the elevator to the lobby. With the secrecy of an espionage plot, the pair persuaded the room clerk to ring Clancy's phone in a few minutes. The hotel employee was advised to inform Clancy that he was working for Boston Garden, it was game time, and the two teams were on the ice ready for the opening face-off.

This accomplished, the culprits returned to their floor and huddled outside Clancy's room. They listened as the phone rang and King screamed in horror. A moment later, Clancy ran out the door, dashed downstairs, and sprinted for the nearest taxicab. He found one and advised the astonished driver that he was none other than King Clancy of the Maple Leafs and was late for his hockey game. The driver happened to be a hockey fan and knew very well that the Bruins match wouldn't start for more than two hours. He asked what Clancy's rush was all about, since the time was only 6:00 P.M.

The truth slowly dawned on King and he ordered the cab stopped. He slowly climbed out and walked back to the hotel, where Day and Conacher awaited him in the lobby. There is no official record of what Clancy said to them, but whatever it was, it could not be printed here.

Such antics, for the most part, were confined to the earlier NHL days when teams played a schedule that was half as long as today's. Teams traveled by train from city to city and enjoyed much more leisure time between matches. Thus, they were able to conduct more pranks than the businesslike jet-flying players of today. Many old-timers, while admitting that the game has become more streamlined and the travel faster, would say that something of the spirit of the early days has been lost in the process.

9. ONCE IN A LIFETIME

Values have changed dramatically in hockey since the advent of the center red line during World War II allowed, for the first time, forward passing all the way to center ice. The once unchallengeable 50-goal mark has been surpassed enough times to make the feat seem almost routine to players like Bobby Hull and Bobby Orr. And now that Phil Esposito and Orr have gone over the 100-point limit, who's to say 150 might not be reached someday? The advent of the forward pass helped speed up play as well as the more recent development of hard slap-shots.

But one record stands with Gibraltar-like firmness in National Hockey League annals—perhaps to last forever. It is a Stanley Cup play-off mark established by the Toronto Maple Leafs in 1942 when the Leafs lost the first three games of the final round to Detroit and then counterattacked to win the next four straight, and capture the Stanley Cup.

No other team has ever been able to take four in a row in a cup round after losing the opening three, and therein lies one of the most dramatic and exciting sagas in Stanley Cup history.

By all sources of logic the Maple Leafs and the Rangers were the two favorites to win the cup that 1941–42 season. The New Yorkers had won the league championship, finishing just three points ahead of second-place Toronto. The Red Wings were a distant fifth, eighteen points behind the Rangers.

But in those days the cup play-downs were constructed so that the first- and second-place teams competed in the first round; the third- and fourth-placers also played off, as did the fifth- and sixth-placers.

As luck would have it, the Rangers were knocked off in six games by the Leafs. Third-place Boston defeated Chicago in a best-of-three-games series and Detroit did the same to the Canadiens. The Red Wings then eliminated Boston in two straight to reach the finals against Toronto.

"We may not have the greatest hockey club in the world," said Red Wing manager Jack Adams before the opening of the finals, "but we're loaded with fighting heart. And if there's anything that wins championships, it's just that."

The Leafs weren't exactly a chicken-livered outfit either. They were led by captain Syl Apps, one of the foremost centers the league has known, they had a crack scorer in Gordie Drillon, and guarding the nets was Turk Broda, regarded as "Mister Clutch" among the goaltending fraternity.

But the Red Wings treated the formidable Leafs with contempt when they met in the opening game on April 4,

1942, at Maple Leaf Gardens. Sid Abel, the present manager of the Red Wings, scored once, and Don "The Count" Grosso got two more as the Detroiters beat Toronto, 3–2, in a surprise upset.

Leaf fans were in for another surprise three nights later when the Detroit club clearly outplayed Toronto for a 4–2 win, again on Maple Leaf Gardens ice. Grosso again scored twice and teammates Mud Bruneteau and Jim Brown each tallied once. The beleaguered Leafs were able to get scores from Sweeney Schriner and defenseman Wally Stanowski, but their big guns, Syl Apps and Gordie Drillon, were silent.

The series shifted to Detroit's Olympia Stadium, and serious observers began to theorize that the Wings were indeed capable of an upset. Jack Adams had a strategy that was proving very successful. There was no center red line in those days, so Adams's plan was to have his players skate with the puck to their own blue line and then skim the rubber into the Toronto defensive zone.

Adams then employed his young, speedier skaters to dash into the Leaf zone and forecheck the Toronto players into errors. "It was not pretty hockey," commented Stanley Cup historian Henry Roxborough, "but it was effective."

The technique was so effective in the third game, on April 9, that the Wings romped to a 5–2 victory. "You got the idea," wrote the late Vern DeGeer, then sports editor of the *Toronto Globe and Mail*, "that it was all over but the shouting."

Detroit fans had plenty to shout about in Olympia Stadium on April 12 because, although the Wings had a 2–0 lead in the second period, the Leafs suddenly rallied and showed the Red Wings they were a team that wouldn't quit. Their renewed determination was due in part to the cunning of their coach, Hap Day.

For one thing, Day had dramatically benched Drillon and aging defenseman Bucko McDonald. He replaced them with two obscure brothers, Nick and Don Metz, and hung his remaining hopes on the effects of a pregame pep talk.

Just before the game Day pulled out a letter he had received from a fourteen-year-old girl. By today's standards the episode that followed would be discounted as pure and unadulterated cornball. But the young fan expressed her conviction that the Leafs would rally and win the cup. There was a special genuineness in her writing that had reached Day, and when he read it to his players it obviously got to them, too.

Sweeney Schriner, an old pro and as hard-bitten as they come, rose when the coach finished reading the letter. "Don't worry about this one, skipper," said Sweeney. "We'll win this one for the little girl."

But Schriner's words seemed meaningless when the scoreboard showed the Wings leading, 2–0, early in the game. Then something happened. Bob Davidson and Lorne Carr each scored for Toronto to tie the score. Although Carl Liscombe put Detroit ahead, 3–2, in the third period, the Leafs' resurgence still worried the Red Wings.

Their fears were justified. Only ten minutes remained when Syl Apps tied the game. Then, to the dismay of Detroit fans, the unknown rookie, Nick Metz, followed with another goal and Toronto pulled out a 4–3 win. But that wasn't the only surprise. The Red Wings, who were a haughty outfit when they led, proceeded to blow their cool. Don Grosso and Eddie Wares charged at referee Mel Harwood and lambasted him for his handling of the game.

With 13,694 fans yelling encouragement, Jack Adams dashed across the ice and threw a punch at Harwood—all this under the gaze of the league president Frank Calder. By this time the fans were so overwrought that they began to threaten Calder, who was thought to be pro-Toronto. Calder required a police escort to escape from the rink.

From his hotel room later that night Calder announced the indefinite suspension of Adams and forbade him from taking any further part in the bench management of the Red Wings. Forward Ebbie Goodfellow would handle the club for the remainder of the play-offs.

Back on their friendly Toronto ice on April 14, the Leafs came on strong. Paced by the new forward line of Apps and the Metz brothers, they routed Detroit, 9–3. Among them they accounted for six goals. The next match, in the Motor City, was just as simple, a 3–0 shutout for Turk Broda that set the stage for the seventh and final game at Maple Leaf Gardens.

By this time the Leafs had generated so much enthusiasm that some 16,218 rooters jammed their way into the arena to set a record for Canada's largest hockey crowd. Naturally, they expected the Leafs to win, and Hap Day's club did not let them down, winning their fourth straight game and the Stanley Cup.

There are several opinions about what part the Red Wings' temper tantrum played in their ultimate demise. Some believe it mattered not one whit, not the way the

Leafs were coming on. Others contend it was the decisive factor that turned the series in Toronto's favor.

"The wild outbursts did not help the morale of the Detroit players," said historian Roxborough, "and neither did the loss of their coach, who had to be replaced by a less experienced leader."

If the Red Wings had maintained their composure there is no question that they would have maintained their edge on Toronto and won the Stanley Cup. In big-league hockey a "cool" club can often defeat a superior team that panics, as the Red Wings did in April, 1942.

10. THE LOOSE GOOSE

For the most part the presidency of the National Hockey League has been a position surrounded by an aura of dignity. During the long reign of Frank Calder from 1917 to 1943 there was little levity associated with NHL's highest office. The same might be said about the years following World War II when Clarence Campbell, former referee, Rhodes scholar, and prosecutor at the Nuremberg war crimes trials, was the NHL president.

But in the short period between the death of Frank Calder in 1943 and the nomination of Clarence Campbell in 1946, there was a rare lightheartedness combined with the efficiency and dedication usually associated with the office. The cause for the change was the personality of Mervyn "Red" Dutton, who was designated president following the death of Frank Calder.

Unlike Calder and Campbell, Dutton, who played for and subsequently ran the New York Americans, was a rollicking type. His good-natured manner, the cockeyed behavior of the Americans, and the generally nutsy world of hockey in New York in the thirties had inured Red to frolicsome behavior. So while he was league president it was not surprising that he became the prime mover in an adventure that involved two newsmen and a very active piece of poultry named Mildred.

Mildred was a pure white goose with a distinctive red beak who, in March, 1943, accomplished what no player, manager, or owner could—she scared the living daylights out of the chief executives of the National and American Hockey Leagues in one night.

The leading characters in what since has become known as "The Case of the Loose Goose" were Red Dutton, John Digby Chick, vice-president of the American Hockey League, and two Toronto sportswriters, Vern DeGeer and Jim Coleman. Oh, yes, and Mildred.

Dutton, an extrovert given to great bursts of enthusiasm, had promised to deliver a dozen ducks to his newspaper admirers after a hunting expedition in western Canada. "Red never delivered," said DeGeer, the late columnist for the *Montreal Gazette,* "so we needled him about the ducks whenever we saw him."

The goading of Dutton became more intense when the Stanley Cup semifinals series between the Toronto Maple Leafs and the Detroit Red Wings opened in Detroit on March 21. By the time the series switched to Toronto, the exasperated Dutton had decided to fulfill his promise.

"He smuggled a dead duck into my suitcase," DeGeer recalled. "When I got home and opened my valise, there was this terrible-looking bird that smelled to high heaven. I thought it was a funny sight, but my wife was madder than a hornet when she saw it. I knew it was Dutton's work so I decided to get even."

Accompanied by *Toronto Globe and Mail* sportswriter Jim Coleman, DeGeer went shopping for another duck at Wasserman's Poultry Market. "I wish to buy a well-plucked duck," DeGeer advised Wasserman.

"I'll tell you what I'm going to do," Wasserman replied. "I'm fresh out of well-plucked ducks, but as a special favor I'm going to let you have a goose. This is an exceptional goose, named Mildred, and I do not wish to kill her. Take her home and she'll outtalk your wife."

Aware that Dutton had checked into the Royal York Hotel, the writers decided to sneak Mildred into the president's suite. "We had Wasserman wrap Mildred up in paper," says DeGeer. "When he got finished, she looked more like a bouquet of flowers than a goose."

Having determined that Dutton was not in his room, Coleman persuaded the assistant manager to give him the NHL president's room key. Meanwhile, Mildred remained silent in her wrapping. "She was perfectly behaved until we got into the elevator," says Coleman, now a columnist for the Southam newspaper chain in Canada. "But the elevator was crowded and, once it started, she stuck out her beak and nudged a stout lady standing directly in front of DeGeer."

The embarrassed DeGeer stuttered an apology, but he was mute when Mildred gave the unsuspecting woman a second nudge and this time accompanied it with a long, low hiss. "The lady turned and gave DeGeer a searching look," says Coleman. "Then she smiled faintly. I attributed the smile to the wartime manpower shortage in Toronto."

When the elevator reached the eleventh floor, DeGeer, perspiring profusely, trotted to Dutton's suite, where he deposited Mildred in the bathtub. He filled the tub with water, drew the shower curtain, and retreated with Coleman to a hiding place in the room closet.

A few hours later, Dutton returned to freshen himself up for the third play-off game that night. "I was half-naked when I walked into the bathroom," says Dutton. "As soon as I started shaving, I heard this strange hissing noise from the bathtub. I pulled aside the curtain and this crazy goose flies at me and out of the room. I was dumbfounded at first, but then I went after it."

There were two doors to the presidential suite, and Mildred chose the one conveniently left open by Coleman and DeGeer. Out flew Mildred, then Dutton, then Coleman and DeGeer. The incredible sight of a red-haired man, clad only in shorts, chasing a goose down the eleventh-floor corridor of the Royal York Hotel, with two men alternately sprinting and howling in pursuit, proved too bewildering for a chambermaid who was walking the other way.

"She became hysterical," DeGeer remembered, "and started screaming. Meanwhile, Dutton was yelling, 'The goose is loose, the goose is loose.' We were afraid of the noise so we gave the chambermaid a dollar and convinced her to be quiet. Finally, Dutton got tired of chasing Mildred and went back to his room."

Within minutes, DeGeer and Coleman recovered Mildred and this time carried her to the room of the late John Digby Chick, a portly gentleman who had left for the Stanley Cup match at the Maple Leaf Gardens. Once again, the writers placed Mildred in a bathtub, provided her with water, and drew the curtain to give her some privacy.

After the game, Chick indulged in a few drinks and returned to his room. "He was feeling very little pain," says Coleman. "After getting into his pajamas, he decided to have a nightcap. He poured a short one and went into the bathroom to add some water."

As he turned on the faucet, Chick felt a pinching sensation on his right thigh. He looked down and observed Mildred leaning out from behind the shower curtain. He stared at her for several seconds, walked back into the bedroom, and stared at the label on his bottle. Assured that it was his regular brand, Chick picked up the telephone and asked for room service. "Please send the house detective to my room," Chick implored. "There's a goose in my bathtub."

The call was transferred to the assistant manager, who was accustomed to dealing with inebriated guests. In a soothing manner, he urged Chick to be calm. "Now, Mr. Chick," he said, "you just climb into bed and you'll find the goose is gone when you wake up in the morning."

The assistant manager's prescription failed to calm Chick. "Either get rid of the goose or me," he demanded. "There'd be three house detectives up here if I had a girl in my bathtub. Get that man up here before I go out in the corridor and start screaming."

Flanked by three house detectives, the assistant manager went up to Chick's room and, sure enough, found Mildred phlegmatically floating in the bathtub. She was removed, amid profuse apologies to Chick, and held in custody overnight at the hotel.

The following day, Mildred was punished for the traumas she had inflicted on the hockey executives. The assistant manager and the house detectives had Mildred for dinner—"but not as a guest," says Coleman. "Chick and Dutton profanely declined an invitation to the banquet."

But Mildred managed to get even with her oppressors, even if she had to do it posthumously. "The assistant manager told me she was the toughest, worst-tasting goose he ever had," says Coleman. "But you couldn't beat her for laughs."

11. THE GREAT GABBO

Eddie Dorohoy, who played for the Montreal Canadiens in post-World War II years, could probably be called the most outspoken player ever to hit the big time. Unfortunately, his gift for gab was greater than his hockey ability.

Dorohoy received his basic training for the National Hockey League in Lethbridge, Alberta, Canada, where he played for a junior team known as the Native Sons. It was there that Dorohoy's vociferousness and his unorthodox behavior on ice became famous—or perhaps infamous— throughout western Canada.

Even when Dorohoy blinked his eyes he seemed to do it in a flamboyant way, and when he took the ice you *knew* he was there. "He played center," said Herb Goren, the former New York Rangers' publicist, "like Connie Mack used to manage his baseball club. He used his stick for directional signals before every face-off, the way Mack waved his scorecard."

Dorohoy was only nineteen years old when the Montreal Canadiens promoted him to the NHL. Normally, a rookie would be awed in the hallowed surroundings of the Canadiens' dressing room, with immortals such as Maurice "Rocket" Richard and Elmer Lach around him. But not Eddie "The Pistol" Dorohoy.

The moment coach Dick Irvin placed the rookie on a line with Lach and Richard, Dorohoy began telling the old masters how the game should be played. On one occasion the three of them were launching a rush during an intrasquad scrimmage when Dorohoy abruptly skidded to a halt and demanded a conference. It was like Jimmy Durante telling the New York Philharmonic to "Stop the music!"—in the middle of Beethoven's Fifth.

Dorohoy somberly called Richard and Lach over to him. "Listen," he said, glaring at the pair as if he was the coach, "the trouble with you guys is that you're out of position."

Irvin, who was watching the episode from the sidelines, nearly fell over backward with laughter at the sight of Dorohoy lecturing his stars. But Dorohoy noticed Irvin out of the corner of his eye and demanded that the coach cease and desist immediately. "What's so funny?" said Dorohoy, reprimanding the senior coach in the league. "Richard and Lach can make mistakes, too. I'm only trying to help them."

Dorohoy wasn't much help to the Canadiens that season. They slumped terribly and Irvin soon became disenchanted with his funnyman. Dick suggested that the 150-pound Dorohoy go on a crash diet to *increase* his weight on the theory that it would help his scoring potential. Eddie managed to stuff himself enough so that he finally reached 162 pounds.

"Now," said Irvin, "you're too fat and soft!"

"The only thing soft," countered Eddie, "is your head."

"Maybe," snapped the coach, "but you're benched."

Even with Dorohoy on the sidelines the Canadiens lost. Irvin was beside himself with rage and wished that he could persuade his gabby forward to learn how to score goals. "Why can't you put that puck in the net?" demanded the exasperated Irvin.

"From the angle on the bench I'm sitting on," quipped Dorohoy with unimpeachable logic, "I'm lucky to touch the puck."

That did it as far as Irvin was concerned. He demoted Dorohoy to the Canadiens' farm team in Dallas, Texas, which was about as far away from Montreal as Irvin could send a player, although Dick thought he could still hear Dorohoy's voice echoing clear across the United States. "Sure, I pop off," Dorohoy agreed, "but I don't say anything malicious. What's the use of living if you can't say what you think?"

Dorohoy eventually wound up playing for Victoria in the Western Hockey League and, if anything, his filibustering increased. "I must be the only hockey player in history," he boasted, "who was ever fined in the summer. Hell, I just took it out of my unemployment insurance."

By the time Eddie was twenty-two years old he had been named coach of the Victoria sextet. That made him one of the youngest coaches of a professional team in any sport and he was favorably compared with baseball's boy managers, Lou Boudreau and Bucky Harris. Unfortunately, the Pistol never enjoyed the same success as his baseball counterparts. Needless to say, it wasn't Dorohoy's fault, and anyone who didn't believe it could quickly find out by asking him. "It was just that I had a bad club," Eddie would explain. "The only thing that improved was my misconduct record."

Dorohoy played for four consecutive years in Victoria and managed to stay among the top three scorers in each of those seasons. By the mid-fifties the New York Rangers were expressing an interest in the young man, and Ranger manager Frank Boucher requested and received permission to invite the Pistol to the New York training camp.

"There were a lot of interesting characters in that camp," recalled Herb Goren. "There was goalie Gump Worsley, and that rugged individualist Lou Fontinato, but for sheer force of personality Dorohoy was easily the 'best of show.' "

Ranger players were as astonished at Dorohoy's audacity as Richard and Lach had been seasons earlier in Montreal. After the Rangers' first workout, Dorohoy clomped into the dressing room, pulled off his white, red, and blue New York jersey, and handed it to trainer Frank Paice. "Here, Paicer," he said, "you can put this in the Hall of Fame."

A few of the Ranger veterans were a trifle annoyed with Dorohoy's braggadocio that day. The upstart deserved some retribution and they were going to provide it. The moment the Pistol left the dressing room, a few of the New Yorkers huddled around Eddie's locker. When Dorohoy returned the next day he picked up his stick and discovered that a puck was taped to the blade—the supreme insult to a hockey player. "It was," said Goren, "the players' way of telling him he couldn't jiggle the disk without losing it."

Eddie laughed it off with a wisecrack: "There wasn't a wing who couldn't score on my line."

In a sense it is unfortunate for the National Hockey League that the fun-loving Dorohoy never became an established fixture in the majors, because he certainly would have added some much-needed humor to the generally overserious NHL scene.

The Rangers hoped he could make it in New York, and Eddie did manage to last with the big club for most of the training camp. He desperately tried to make an impression on management, even if it meant challenging men nearly twice his weight.

One night the Rangers were playing an exhibition in Eddie's old stamping grounds of Victoria. During the match Dorohoy clashed with Colin Kilburn of the Victoria sextet. Kilburn was considerably heavier than Dorohoy, yet Eddie not only held his own but managed to outbox Kilburn and finally knocked his old teammate to the ice. And, when Kilburn was down, Dorohoy got to his knees and continued throwing punches from the semireclining position. All this was for the benefit of Ranger coach Muzz Patrick. "I just wanted to be sure," said Dorohoy, "that Muzz wasn't underrating me."

Patrick didn't underrate him as a fighter, but he had his doubts about Dorohoy as a hockey player, so Eddie the Pistol, alias "The Great Gabbo," finished his career with his major-league humor confined to the minor leagues.

12. THE BATTLE OF
   THE BULGE

In 1947, 1948, and 1949 the Toronto Maple Leafs, coached by Clarence "Hap" Day and managed by Conn Smythe, had won an unprecedented three Stanley Cup championships, and naturally were favored to win again in 1950. But the vitriolic Smythe was worried. He was fearful that his players were becoming too complacent and too fat.

Smythe's fears were confirmed early in the 1949–50 season when the Leafs opened their campaign with the vigor of a pricked balloon. Smythe was puzzled, so he studied the slumping Toronto sextet throughout November. Finally, on November 30, Smythe, a veteran of World Wars I and II, opened what became known as hockey's classic "Battle of the Bulge."

Headlines in the Toronto newspapers screamed the news: SMYTHE READS THE RIOT ACT TO LEAFS. Al Nickleson, who at the time was covering the Leafs for the *Globe and Mail*, said, "The fiery president blasted the fat men on the team. That was the beginning of his 'Battle of the Bulge.' "

Although Smythe singled out defenseman Garth Boesch and forwards Howie Meeker, Harry Watson, Vic Lynn, and Sid Smith for his blasts, the key target of Smythe's ire was his longtime goaltending stalwart, Walter "Turk" Broda. Turk had earned his nickname as a junior player because his neck always turned crimson when he got excited, which was often. Now Smythe was giving Broda something to get really red-necked about.

"It's condition that's needed," Smythe demanded. "Nothing but condition. If it isn't Turk's fault, we'll find out whose it is."

Smythe's opening gun in "The Battle of the Bulge" was a demand that his players reduce their weight to specified limits. Broda, who weighed 197 pounds, was ordered to lose 7 pounds. To underline the seriousness of his offensive, Smythe promptly called up reserve goalie Gil Mayer from his Pittsburgh farm team. "We're starting Mayer in our next game," Smythe asserted, "and he'll stay in here even if the score is five hundred to one against the Leafs—and I don't think it will be."

This was the supreme insult to Broda, who, except for a stint in the army, had never missed a game during his twelve seasons as a Toronto goalie. But Smythe was unimpressed. It was Tuesday and he was giving Turk until Saturday to fulfill the demand. "I'm taking Broda out of the nets," Smythe said, "and he's not going back until he shows some common sense. Two seasons ago he weighed 185. Last season he went up to 190—and now this. A goalie has to have fast reflexes, and you can't move fast when you're overweight."

Then Smythe directed his wrath toward the other culprits. "We have the best hockey public in the world and we're going to dish out the hockey it wants to see. If the players don't come through, they won't be traded. They'll sit on the bench. I'm not going to let them loaf at the expense of some other teams. We'll let them try buying their own roast beef for a change."

Smythe's outburst reverberated across Canada and parts of the United States, and soon "The Battle of the Bulge" became a *cause célèbre*. Neutral observers regarded Turk's tussle with the scales as a huge joke, win or lose, but to the Toronto boss it was no joke. None of the Leafs was particularly amused, either.

Toronto restaurant owner Sam Shopsowitz took an ad in the local papers, declaring, "For that 'Old Broda' look, eat at Shopsy's." Another featured a caricature of Broda stopping eight pucks at once with the caption: "Just three weeks ago I was the best goalkeeper in the league. If I'd only eaten a few more king-sized steaks at the Palisades I'd be fat enough to fill the whole net and they would never score on me!"

Meanwhile, reporters were following Broda's hour-by-hour fight against fat with utter fascination. The *Globe and Mail* featured a photograph of him sitting in a steam bath with a doleful Jack Benny look on his face and a towel draped around his head like a turban. "It seems to me I've been eating nothing but apples," Turk was saying, "and killing my thirst with oranges. For my evening meal I had a lean steak and spinach. No potatoes, no bread. And a cup of tea. No cream, no sugar."

After one day of severe dieting, Turk trimmed his weight from 197 to 193 and all of Canada seemed to breathe easier. Even so, by midweek Broda had still not reached his approved weight limit and Smythe dropped another bombshell. He sent five players as well as cash "in five figures" to Cleveland for tall, twenty-three-year-old goalie Al Rollins. According to hockey experts, Rollins was the best professional goalie outside the National Hockey League, and he was to prove that in years to come. The acquisition of Rollins emphasized the gravity of Broda's position. "I don't blame Mr. Smythe," Turk said. "I guess we had to learn the hard way."

To which Smythe replied, "If Turk makes 190 pounds and makes the team, he can play. We'll do everything in our power to have him out there until the last button pops off his vest. But as far as I'm concerned, the team will come before manager, coach, or any player. Turk's done a great deal for us, and we're not forgetting that. But we've done a great deal to make Turk a great goalie, too. Nothing would give me more pleasure than to see him get down in weight, get his timing back, and see the team fighting to keep him in there."

Turk and his wife, Betty, were besieged by advice and well-wishes from people all over Canada. A well-known nutritionist advised that the way to lose weight was by will-power. "Overweight," he told the rotund goalie, "is caused solely by eating more food than is needed." One woman phoned Mrs. Broda and told her that she had lost twenty-eight pounds in two weeks. She promised to forward her diet to the Brodas.

Smythe had set the final weigh-in for Saturday afternoon, prior to the evening match against the New York Rangers at Maple Leaf Gardens. He refused to divulge what specific action he would take against Broda, or the other Leafs, but suggested that it wouldn't be very lenient. "I think that's my business," Smythe asserted. "But I might fine them $500."

As the indicted players approached the homestretch, they all appeared to be losing the stipulated pounds, but they were suffering in the process. Harry Watson, who had shed nine pounds, four more than he was supposed to, said he was too weak to report to the gymnasium on Friday afternoon. Defenseman Garth Boesch said he was so hungry he could eat dogmeat. And Broda, forcing a laugh, announced, "I'm so thirsty I could drink a rinkful of water."

The climax of the weeklong calorie crusade finally arrived on Saturday afternoon when, one by one, the penitent Leafs stepped on the scales under Smythe's watchful eye. Watson, Boesch, Lynn, Smith, and Meeker all weighed in under the limit. Finally it was Broda's turn.

Turk moved forward and gingerly placed his feet on the platform. The numbers finally settled—just under 190 pounds. He had made it! If Turk was delighted, Smythe was doubly enthused because he regarded his goaltender with paternal affection. "There may be better goalies around somewhere," said the manager, "but there's no greater sportsman than the Turkey. If the Rangers score on him tonight, I should walk out and hand him a malted milk, just to show I'm not trying to starve him to death."

That night the Maple Leaf Gardens was packed with 13,359 Turk-rooters, and when the former fat man skated out for the opening face-off, the Gardens regimental band swung into "Happy Days Are Here Again" and followed that with a chorus of "She's Too Fat for Me."

Finally, referee George Gravel dropped the puck to

start the game, and the Rangers immediately swarmed in on Broda. This time, however, he was the Turk of old. "He never looked better," said *Toronto Globe and Mail* sports editor Jim Vipond. "He moved side to side in front of his netted bastion to block the best efforts of the Rangers."

Unfortunately, Broda's slimmer teammates couldn't beat goalie Chuck Rayner of the Rangers and the first period ended with the teams tied, 0–0. And it was the same story in the second period as each team desperately probed for an opening. The Rangers ultimately got the big break late in the middle period when Pentti Lund bisected the Toronto defense and moved within eyeball-to-eyeball distance of Broda. Lund found his opening and fired the puck mightily, but somehow Broda thrust his pad in the way and deflected the rubber out of danger. To a man, the fans rose and toasted Turk with a standing ovation, and when the second period ended, the contest remained a scoreless deadlock.

Early in the third period the Leafs were attempting a change in lines when Howie Meeker and Vic Lynn, two of the marked fat men, combined to feed a lead pass to Max Bentley, who normally wouldn't have been on the ice with them. Bentley dipsy-doodled through the Ranger checkers and unleashed a steaming shot that flew past Rayner. Later in the period another fat man, Harry Watson, skimmed a pass to Bill Ezinicki, who beat Rayner.

Now all eyes were on the clock as it ticked toward the twenty-minute mark and the end of the game. With only a minute remaining, Broda still had a shutout. The countdown began: ten, nine, eight seconds . . . the crowd was on its feet . . . seven, six, five . . . they were roaring as if the

Leafs had won the Stanley Cup ... four, three, two, one. The game was over! Turk dove for the puck and gathered it in. It was his symbolic trophy for winning "The Battle of the Bulge."

Surrounded by jubilant players in the dressing room, Broda was embraced by Smythe and his new understudy, Al Rollins. He stepped on the scales and discovered that he had lost 4 more pounds during the heat of the game. He was now down to 186 and raring to go through the season's campaign.

Broda played some of the best goal of his life that year and finished the season with a commendable 2.45 goals against average. The following year he split the goaltending job with Rollins. Turk played in thirty-one games and compiled a 2.19 average, while Rollins played in forty games and delivered an extraordinary 1.75 mark. The combined Leaf total was 1.97, and the Broda-Rollins team won the Vezina Trophy for the best goaltending in the league.

A few days after Turk had won "The Battle of the Bulge," he was humorously quoted by a Toronto writer: "Some day I'm going to write my memoirs and I'll write the real reason why I got my weight down below 190 pounds. The real reason is that I was afraid that if I *didn't* get down to 190 pounds Coach Day would have made me sleep in an upper berth on the road trips."

13. LEONE'S MAGIC ELIXIR

A novice fan might find it hard to believe, but late in the 1950–51 season the hottest hockey items in New York City consisted of a strange liquid known as Leone's Magic Elixir and a *World-Telegram* sportswriter named Jim Burchard. During the season, life had become difficult for the New York Rangers. Their record was well below .500 by early December and unless some sort of miracle could be produced, the future appeared bleak. Gene Leone, an affable restaurateur and ardent Ranger fan, pondered the ingredients in his kitchen one day and suddenly an idea hit him. He'd distill some of his delectable juices, mix them with vintage wine from his cellar, and produce a "wonder drink" for the Rangers. It would be good publicity for Leone and perhaps it would boost his favorite team's sagging spirits.

Just before Christmas, Leone perfected his formula and poured it into a large black bottle about three times the size of a normal whiskey bottle. With appropriate fuss

73

and fanfare, "Leone's Magic Elixir" was carried into the Ranger dressing room, where such heroes as Don "Bones" Raleigh, Pentti Lund, Frankie Eddolls, Neil Colville, and Zellio Toppazzini quaffed the brew.

To say the results were amazing would be an understatement. They were hallucinatory. After drinking the mixture the Rangers began to win and win and win. By early January they had lost only two of their eleven games, but observers insisted the real test would come when the Blueshirts visited Toronto, where they hadn't had a victory for ages.

Now the fun started. Leone demanded that the magic elixir, whose formula was so secret that he wouldn't even trust it to paper, be prepared at the last possible moment. This was done on Saturday afternoon. When the elixir was ready, he turned it over to Jim Burchard, who boarded a plane for Toronto. The plan was for Jim to arrive just before game time and present the potion to the Rangers.

Wearing his traditional black hat with its big brim turned down on each side, Burchard boarded the plane carrying a sealed bag containing the bottle of elixir surrounded by three hot-water bottles. A skull and crossbones adorned the black zippered bag.

Unknown to the Ranger strategists, the Maple Leaf organization was arranging for the Canadian customs agent to seize the black bottle at Toronto Airport, denying its use to the New Yorkers. "Naturally," wrote Al Nickleson in the *Toronto Globe and Mail*, "the Leafs had been hoping the flagon would have been seized as an enemy power when Burchard wouldn't explain its contents."

But according to Nickleson, a *Globe* photographer named Harold Robinson saved the Rangers "by undermining the customs officer with stale jokes and Christmas cigars so that Burchard had no trouble slipping by." Then Robinson pushed Burchard into his car and set several Ontario speed records driving to Maple Leaf Gardens just in time for the quaffing.

Burchard had forgotten a corkscrew, so he had to push the cork down into the bottle. The Rangers, who actually detested the vile stuff, had their brief sips—some just gargled and spat it out—and then returned it to Burchard.

"When the cork stops disintegrating," explained Burchard as he poured what the Rangers couldn't drink down the sink, "we know that the stuff has lost its power. Why, look at that! Here comes a mouse up the drain waving a white flag."

The Rangers, who enjoyed the joke more than the elixir itself, had their laughs and then went out on the ice and performed like supermen. Within seven minutes of the first period they scored three goals and coasted to a 4–2 win.

Their victory caused a sensation. "CAMERAMAN LUGS FLAGITIOUS FLAGON," screamed a headline in the *Globe and Mail*. "RANGERS NEW AID SCORNED BY LEAFS," the *Toronto Telegram* roared. While players and scientists speculated on the elixir's contents, Leone said he'd bottle the stuff and sell it commercially.

"It tasted like the Atlantic Ocean," said photographer Robinson. "I think it's hot broth," said Leaf coach Joe Primeau. The Rangers had other opinions that are not fit to print, but the idea was appropriately conveyed by Toronto writer Bob Hesketh, who tasted the stuff. "It was a creamy liquid," said Hesketh, "that smelled just like water doesn't."

Occasionally, Leone would be distracted by business and forget to distill the potion. Once, when the Rangers lost to Detroit, Burchard explained, "The Leone brew wasn't on deck. Without it, the Rangers were under a psychological handicap."

After the loss, an SOS was dispatched to Leone, who quickly prepared more of the liquid, and the Rangers whipped Toronto, 2–1, the next night.

And so it went. Two weeks later, Burchard arrived in Toronto without the bottle and the Rangers lost. The papers attributed the loss to the missing elixir. Leone soon produced more, though, and it seemed to keep the Rangers in contention for a while longer. But the psychological value of the elixir had run its course and the Blueshirts faded into fifth place at the end of the season. The "elixir" that the Rangers really needed was in the form of good coaching and better players. Unfortunately, the New York sextet rarely obtained the formula. In fact, the Rangers have only reached the Stanley Cup finals once since the New Yorkers last won the cup in 1940. But that one effort—during the 1949–50 season—still is regarded as a hockey classic.

14. THEY DIDN'T KNOW WHEN TO QUIT

Upsets are a dime a dozen in hockey. But one of the most unusual occurred when the Rangers entered the Stanley Cup finals in April, 1950. That Blueshirt club was a leathery outfit—not as big, well balanced, or rambunctious as other Stanley Cup contenders, but a capable crew. The team had stalwart forwards, including Pentti Lund, Tony Leswick, and Edgar Laprade; hefty defensemen like Gus Kyle, Jack Lancien, and Allan Stanley; and an adroit goaltender, "Bonnie Prince Charles" Rayner.

In the semifinal round the Rangers upset the Montreal Canadiens, who were armed with Rocket Richard, Bill Durnan, and Butch Bouchard, by defeating them 3–0 in the fifth and final game on Montreal ice. The winning goal had been scored by a baby-faced rookie named Jack Gordon, now coach of the Minnesota North Stars.

Gordon had tears in his eyes that night in the Ranger dressing room as teammates hoisted him to their shoulders. Ranger coach Lynn Patrick managed to pull himself out of his state of euphoric shock for a moment to tell the press, "Why, if the boys can keep the sharp edge, we're a cinch to take the Stanley Cup."

As much as they admired him, newsmen took Lynn and his prediction lightly. And for good reason. The Ringling Brothers Barnum and Bailey Circus already had camped in Madison Square Garden, compelling the Rangers to play *all* their "home" games on the road. To make matters worse their opponents were the awesome Detroit Red Wings.

In fact, the Rangers were nearly wiped off the ice in the opening game of the finals. The Red Wings romped to a 4–1 win at Detroit's Olympia Stadium. Patrick was furious. He blamed the loss on overconfidence and announced that he had promoted his lilliputian goalie, Emile Francis, from New Haven to the Ranger roster in case he was needed. (In 1964 the tiny net minder became general manager-coach of the Rangers.)

The second and third games were held on neutral ice or, if you will, Ranger "home" ice—Maple Leaf Gardens in Toronto. All tickets were sold forty-five minutes after they went on sale, which says it all for Toronto as a hockey town. After the two games in Toronto, all the other games were slated to be played in Detroit.

Maple Leaf Gardens was not expected to make playing any easier for the Blueshirts, and Red Wing coach Tommy Ivan sensed trouble. "It'll be tough for us," he said before the second game of the series. "I'm still scared of them. The series will go more than four games." Ivan didn't realize how prophetic he was.

The Rangers whomped the Red Wings in the second game, 3–1, on two goals by Laprade and another by defenseman Pat Egan, and tied the finals at one game apiece. What's more, the supposedly neutral Toronto fans adopted the Rangers as their own and rooted for New York as passionately as they would have for the Leafs. But they had little to cheer about in the third game, played at the Gardens. Detroit blanked the Rangers, 4–0, and returned to Olympia expecting an early trip to Florida to celebrate their play-off win. The Wings had good cause for optimism; they led the series, two games to one, and all the remaining games would be played on friendly Detroit ice. "We'll win the next two games and wind this series up in a hurry," the Wings promised their fans.

The promise began to crumble at the end of the second period of the fourth game with the Wings ahead, 2–0. Ranger Buddy O'Connor scored to make it 2–1. Although Detroit scored early in the third period, the Rangers were carrying a hot hand. Ranger Edgar Laprade made it 3–2 at 8:09 and Gus Kyle tied the game at 16:26 of the period, setting the stage for sudden-death overtime. Here's how *New York Times* writer Joe Nichols described the early overtime action:

"The Rangers tried to keep up their heavy rushes, but the Wings took over and thrice sent their star pointmaker, Ted Lindsay, in on Rayner. Two of his drives were easy enough, but the third seemed to have him beaten and only a miraculous save kept the disk out of the cage."

Then the Rangers counterattacked. Ed Slowinski robbed Detroit's Joe Carveth of the puck behind the Red Wing net. He skimmed a pass to Don "Bones" Raleigh twenty feet in front of the cage. The bean pole center was checked by defenseman Jack Stewart and started to fall as the puck reached him. But he took a desperate backhand swipe at it and fell on his stomach, his eyes riveted on the net.

Somehow the puck skidded to goalie Harry Lumley's right. The big net minder flashed out his right skate, but the rubber eluded the goalie's blade, hit the goalpost, and went into the net at 8:34 of the sudden-death overtime, tying the series, two games to two. "No one in the place expected Raleigh to touch the puck, much less score," observed Bill Lauder, Jr., in the *New York Herald-Tribune*.

When it was over, Patrick admitted that Raleigh had had no business being on the ice at the time. "He was so tired," said Lynn, "I wanted to keep him off, but Nick Mickoski had just been hurt, so I had no choice. I needed bodies and I got a goal."

The Rangers prepared for the fifth game of the tied series with the grim specter of injuries clouding their camp. Mickoski had suffered a dislocated shoulder and Gordon was lost for the rest of the series with torn knee ligaments. And, of course, there was the problem of playing another game at unfriendly Olympia.

No matter. Game five was on, and the Rangers went out and took a 1–0 lead on Dunc Fisher's goal at 7:44 of the second period, then saw the lead evaporate with less than two minutes remaining in the game when Ted Lindsay sank his own rebound. But the Rangers treated Lindsay's goal as an idle annoyance, particularly when Bones Raleigh, on a pass from Ed Slowinski, saved the game for the Blueshirts during overtime.

The speed of Raleigh's goal arrested the imagination of the 12,610 spectators. The play had evolved with only a minute and a half gone in the overtime. Slowinski captured the puck behind the net and fed Raleigh, who unleashed a ten-foot shot that found an opening between Lumley's pads.

"Eddie did all the work," Raleigh insisted. "It was the best pass I've ever had." So now New York led the series, three games to two, and needed but one win in the next two games to take the cup.

The sixth, and what Ranger followers believed would be the last, game of the series was held at Olympia on Saturday, April 22, 1950. To many observers it should have been the grand finale, and those who saw the game or heard New York broadcaster Bert Lee describe it on the radio still have difficulty believing that the Rangers ultimately lost.

The tragedy developed rather unexpectedly, for in the first period, before the Red Wings could find their groove, the Rangers had built a lead on goals by Stanley and Fisher. Lindsay reduced the lead by one in the period's final minute, but Lund scored after three minutes of the second period to put New York ahead by two. Again the Red Wings retaliated, scoring late in the second period, and the Rangers went ahead again in the third on a goal by Tony Leswick.

But the fact was, there was too much Lindsay for the Rangers. The ubiquitous left wing stickhandled through three Rangers to score at 4:13. Then Sid Abel scored later in the game after snaring his own rebound in front of Rayner.

After a disappointing loss for the Rangers, it was time for the climactic event, the final game on April 23 at

Olympia. For the first two periods it appeared that the Rangers had the Stanley Cup in the bag. Goals by Stanley and Leswick gave them a 2–0 lead after the first period. Detroit tied it in the second at 2–2, but O'Connor put New York ahead again at 11:42 of the middle period.

That was the Ranger's last moment to exult in a lead. Shortly thereafter Jim McFadden beat Stanley to the puck and shot an "impossible" angled shot past Rayner to tie the score. There was nothing left but excruciating overtime—the first goal deciding the game and the cup winner. "You could see it coming," said Patrick. "Once the overtime started I figured we were through. The boys just had nothing left."

Well, not quite nothing. The Rangers traded blow for blow, shot for shot with the Red Wings in the hostile Olympia Stadium for twenty minutes of the first sudden death and very nearly won the cup. A shot by Mickoski had Lumley beaten, but the puck hit the goalpost and went in the wrong direction.

By the second overtime the Rangers were still there, but they were tiring fast and the end was near. "The Wings had carried the play to the fading Blueshirts," wrote Lew Walter in the *Detroit Times*, "and had missed goals by hairline margins."

Detroit's George Gee was one who barely missed scoring the winning goal. He was put in the clear by Pete Babando. Rayner moved slowly out of his cage, ten, twelve, fifteen feet. Gee shot. Rayner sprawled and smothered the puck. Referee Bill Chadwick (who later became the television "color" announcer for Ranger home games) whistled a face-off in deep Ranger zone, to the left of the net.

Patrick sent out Buddy O'Connor, Alex Kaleta, Nick Mickoski, Pat Egan, and Allan Stanley. Detroit's unit consisted of Gee, Babando, Doc Couture, Leo Reise, and Marcel Pronovost. Gee was to take the face-off against O'Connor. The Red Wing paused and skated back to Babando. "Move over behind me," Gee said. "You're too far to the left." His words proved to be insightful.

"I moved over," Babando said later. "I still wasn't far enough, because Gee beat O'Connor to the draw and whipped the puck back to my right. I had to reach for it to catch it on my backhand."

More than eight minutes had ticked away in the second sudden death when Gee won the draw. Rayner was at the near corner of the net as the puck moved toward Babando. The Ranger goalie's view was obscured by Stanley, his defenseman. "When the puck hit my stick," Babando recalled, "I just let fly through the scramble. I wasn't sure the shot was on the net." It was.

The puck took off along a straight line two feet off the ice. It flitted past Gee, past Stanley, and past Couture toward a three-foot opening at the right corner. Rayner knew the shot was coming but he couldn't find the puck because of the forest of bodies in front of him. "I never saw it coming," said Rayner. At the last second he fell to the ice kicking out his left pad in a spread-eagle split. But he felt nothing hit his pads.

Intuitively, his head turned back to the left—toward the net. The puck was there in the corner, along with the Rangers' shattered dreams.

When the cheering had subsided and the Rangers had wiped away their tears, Red Wing captain Sid Abel walked into the New York dressing room and gave the Blueshirts the finest testimonial they could have received, short of winning the cup. Abel pumped Rayner's hand, looked around the room, and said to the other exhausted New Yorkers, "Don't you guys ever know when to quit?"

15. A GOALTENDER'S LIFE IS . . .

It has been said, with some justification, that a young man has to be at least slightly crazy to pursue a career as a goaltender. The reasons are obvious. The goaltender stands in front of a net six feet wide by four feet high and attempts to prevent a six-ounce piece of hard vulcanized rubber from flying past him. What makes this an exceptionally difficult operation is that the puck often flies at speeds of about 120 miles per hour, making it practically invisible to the goalie.

Many contemporary hockey people are inclined to believe that the present-day fire-wagon brand of hockey is fraught with more problems for a goaltender than the slower-paced game of yesteryear. Old-timers such as Johnny Gottselig, who played for the Black Hawks in the thirties, would not necessarily agree to that. Gottselig remembers goaltender Charlie Gardiner's death in 1934 two months after the Hawks won their first Stanley Cup. "Chuck was in his prime when he died," said Gottselig.

"It was only his sixth season in the league. I think his whole life was shortened by goaltending. He was always alone. . . . Goalies are probably the loneliest guys in the world."

Not every goaltender who entered the National Hockey League has been a solitary introvert. The Maple Leafs' Turk Broda was a gregarious, fun-loving type who enjoyed a joke as much as the next fellow, although quite often the joke was on him.

Turk was first scouted by the Detroit Red Wings and invited to their training camp in the 1934–35 season. "He still had hay behind his ears," said veteran Lorne Duguid, "and he was an inviting target for dressing room fun." What made Broda such an obvious target was his raucous blue serge suit with white stripes, which made him look like a zebra.

Unknown to Broda, the Red Wings' activities were closely followed that season by a tailor who happened to be a fanatic hockey fan. The tailor showed up for Detroit scrimmages and occasionally did some work for the players. One afternoon, while Broda was on the ice practicing, the tailor arrived in the Red Wing dressing room and asked Duguid if there was any work to be done.

Thinking fast—not to mention sadistically—Duguid walked over to Broda's locker and picked up Turk's blue serge suit. With a straight face, Duguid advised the tailor that he had hurriedly bought the suit and to his dismay discovered that the pants were much too long. "Do me a favor?" Duguid asked. "Shorten these about ten inches and bring them back within the hour because I have a date tonight."

The obliging tailor went to work on the pants and

completed the operation long before Broda ended his workout. "As he climbed into his trousers," recalled Vern DeGeer, the *Montreal Gazette's* columnist, "Broda let out a scream of anguish. The tailor had shortened them so that the cuffs ended halfway between his ankles and his knees."

Desperate to conceal his embarrassing appearance, Broda loosened his suspenders hoping to lengthen the pants. But that only succeeded in dropping the waistline down around his hips, which was as offensive looking as the short trouser legs. "He was like an old-fashioned gal in hobble skirts," said DeGeer.

Duguid looked on with an expression of sympathy on his face. He had thought that the tailor would merely tuck the extra material up the underside of the pants. But on closer inspection Duguid discovered that he had actually cut off the material, leaving Broda no opportunity for readjustment.

"It was the most expensive gag I ever pulled," Duguid admitted. "I suddenly realized it was the only suit of clothes Turk had. So I had to loan him a pair of my trousers, and then take him downtown and buy him a new suit."

When Broda enlisted in the Canadian Army in 1943, during World War II, he was succeeded by a tall, gaunt-looking young man named Frank McCool. A scholarly type, McCool eventually left hockey to become a journalist. By 1954 he had become the sports editor of the *Calgary Albertan,* which seemed to justify his decision to quit goaltending at a relatively early age.

"I quit early," said McCool, "mainly because of ulcers. Why I had ulcers I don't know, but it didn't help being a goalie. It's the toughest, most unappreciated job in sports. The goalie always takes the rap. It's always his fault when you lose. The crowd gets on you and then the papers pick it up. Soon the players themselves begin to think you're to blame."

For McCool, the strain was mental. For other goaltenders, the physical punishment can tire them and inspire them to hang up their pads. One of the first of the really great goalies to succumb to exhaustion was Clint "Benny" Benedict, who broke in as a pro in 1913 with the Ottawa Senators. "After the first couple of seasons," said Benedict, "I lost count of the stitches they put in my head. They didn't have a goal crease in those days and the forwards would come roaring right in and bang you as hard as they could. If they knocked you down you were supposed to get back on your feet before you could stop the puck—those were the rules."

A strapping six-footer, Benedict absorbed terrific punishment for eighteen years. Obviously his sturdy physique was an asset to his playing longevity. "I remember," he once said, "at least four times being carried into the dressing room to get all stitched up and then going back in to play. There were some other times, too, but I don't remember them."

Benedict ranked with Georges Vezina, George Hainsworth, and other of the early great goaltenders. He played on five Stanley Cup champion teams, four of them in Ottawa, and appeared in thirty-two Stanley Cup games. But one of his signal contributions to the art of goaltending was his innovative decision to fall to the ice in order to block a shot. Until Benedict came along, it had been traditional for goaltenders to remain upright throughout the game.

"It actually was against the rules to fall to the ice," Benny explained. "But if you made it look like an accident you could get away without a penalty. I got pretty good at it and soon all the other goalies were doing the same thing. I guess you could say we all got pretty good at it about 1914, and the next season the league had to change the rule."

Benedict's revolutionary maneuver was greeted with the same hostility as Jacques Plant's decision to wander out of his net would be when he joined the Montreal Canadiens in the fifties. The first time Benedict displayed his flopping style in Toronto, the fans shouted, "Bring your bed, Benny!"

There are those who say that Benedict single-handedly won the 1923 edition of the Stanley Cup for Ottawa. The Senators were playing Vancouver for the title, and in the final game of the series Ottawa was nursing a 2–1 lead with only three minutes remaining in the contest.

At this point the Senators were penalized twice in succession and had to defend against the determined Vancouver club with only three skaters to the home team's five. It was Benedict who now rose to the challenge and blunted every one of the enemy's dangerous thrusts. "We were out on our feet at the end," Clint said, "but we won."

Significantly, it was not long afterward that New York Ranger manager Lester Patrick defined the importance of a goaltender to a hockey club. "The goalie," said Patrick, "is seventy percent of a team's strength. A good one can make a weak team awfully tough to beat. A mediocre one will ruin his team."

Ironically, Patrick later was to feel personally the truth of his analysis. For during World War II the Rangers had a mediocre team and some of the worst goaltenders hockey has seen. One of them was Ken McAuley, who was in the nets one night against the Red Wings and lost the game, 15–0, a record that still stands.

Two decades later the Rangers were to exact sweet revenge against the Red Wings for that shellacking in a strange episode at Madison Square Garden. It was late March, 1962, and the Rangers and Red Wings were neck and neck in a race for the fourth and final play-off berth. Each team had fifty-seven points for the season, and the two points that would go to the winner of the upcoming game would just about clinch fourth place, which would be the final play-off berth.

It promised to be an extraordinary game for many reasons. Doug Harvey, the Rangers' rookie coach, was also taking a regular turn on defense and, despite his advanced age, was playing like an all-star. What's more, the usually downtrodden Rangers were making one of their rare bids for a play-off position. New York's captain, Andy Bathgate, led the league in scoring with a small margin over Bobby Hull of the Chicago Black Hawks, and Gordie Howe, the immense Detroit right wing, was aiming for his five hundredth NHL goal.

The game that developed into one of the most exciting ever played on Madison Square Garden ice started with the stickhandling magic of Bathgate, who sidestepped his way around the Red Wing defense and scored on a fifteen-foot shot that Detroit goalie Hank Bassen failed to handle. But before the first period ended, Howe skimmed a pass to linemate Claude Laforge, who beat Ranger goalie Lorne "Gump" Worsley.

With the score tied, 1–1, in the second period, Howe took command. The Red Wings were short one man (Laforge was in the penalty box) when Howe captured the puck at center ice and loped toward the Ranger zone. "Only one defender stood in his path," said Ken Rudeen of *Sports Illustrated,* "and that man was Harvey, the greatest defenseman in hockey."

Howe has always had the extraordinary knack of appearing to be doing nothing very much at the precise moment he is executing an extremely intricate maneuver. This time he innocently approached the waiting Harvey and moved calmly to the right. Suddenly Howe jerked his body to the left in an apparent drive for the other side of Harvey. But it was only the old pro's feint. Interpreting the move a split second too late, Harvey tried to thwart Howe with a thrust of his extended hip. He did manage to graze the onrushing Red Wing, but not hard enough to drop Howe to the ice. Gordie regained his equilibrium and, with his stick and puck to the right of his body, moved in on the crouched Worsley.

Quite properly, the goalie expected a backhand shot— except that Howe was the only player in the league who could shoot ambidextrously, and Gordie quickly switched hands, moving the puck and stick to his left. Before the goaltender could move, Howe had shot the puck past him for his five hundredth goal and a 2–1 lead for Detroit.

The Rangers weren't about to capitulate, Howe or no Howe. Before the second period ended, they tied the score, 2–2, thus setting the stage for one of the most freakish episodes in hockey. It developed late in the third period with the teams still in the death grip of a deadlocked match and no break in sight.

With the redheaded Bassen playing one of his better games at the Detroit goal cage, the Rangers launched a particularly threatening attack. Bathgate and his longtime sidekick, Dean Prentice, moved over the Detroit blue line as the Red Wing defense slipped out of position. Prentice caressed the puck on his stick along the left side of the ice, but appeared to have no better than a five-to-one chance of beating Bassen from this relatively difficult angle.

However, Bassen had a reputation for impetuous moves. He often left the goal crease to engage in fights and was notorious for wandering far out of the net after stray pucks. This, however, was no time for playing around.

For reasons known best to himself, Bassen skated ten feet forward and confronted Prentice head on. At the moment it seemed to be a brilliant riposte, for the Ranger was forced farther and farther from the net. Then the unbelievable happened.

Bassen's stick left his right hand, slid across the ice, hit the black-taped blade of Prentice's stick, knocked the puck harmlessly into the corner of the rink, and sent Prentice crashing into the boards. For most onlookers it was difficult to determine whether Bassen had panicked, had deliberately planned to release his stick, or had accidentally let it slip out of his thick leather gauntlet. Certainly it would be an enormously difficult call for a referee. But the rule book clearly states that the fouled player in such a situation should be awarded a penalty shot, which amounts to a clear, unimpeded play on the goalkeeper. The referee blew his whistle and, to the complete dismay of the Red Wings, ordered that a penalty shot be awarded.

This, in and of itself, was a rarity. There had not been a penalty shot called at Madison Square Garden for six years, and only nine had been called in the league throughout the 1961–62 season. But there was no mistaking the fact that Prentice had been fouled and had the right to take the prize.

At this point still another extraordinary thing happened. The referee designated Bathgate as the man to take the shot. This might have been legal had Prentice been disabled on the play, but Dean was fully recovered from his crash into the boards and joined his teammates on the sidelines as Bathgate accepted the puck at center ice in preparation for his one-on-one foray against Bassen.

The play would be worth $100,000 to the Rangers, and as much as $300,000 in total prize money if they went on to win the Stanley Cup. "To the crowd," said Rudeen, "it was like watching the clash of cobra and mongoose. The broad expanse of white ice was empty except for the two opposing players. The crowd hushed. The referee blew his whistle."

One of the most perceptive players in the league, Bathgate was well aware of Bassen's strengths and weaknesses. He was particularly conscious of the goalie's impulsiveness, so Bathgate decided to take advantage of that flaw in Bassen's style. At center ice the Ranger captain carefully pushed the puck ahead of him, seemingly in slow motion. Gradually, he picked up speed as he passed over the Detroit blue line, one eye on the puck, the other studying Bassen for the crucial move that would suggest the goaltender's strategy.

Bassen did precisely what Bathgate had hoped he would do—the goalie moved forward out of his crease, leaving enough room for the Ranger ace to toy with his foe. Bathgate's first ploy was a drop of his shoulder, suggesting a move to the right side of the net. The Detroiter fell for the trick so easily that it appeared he was being pulled away from the goal by invisible strings. While Bassen was falling hopelessly into Bathgate's trap, the Ranger casually moved to his left and backhanded the puck into the yawning net.

The controversial goal gave the Rangers the game and fourth place. Yet to this day Bassen and the Red Wings could rightfully claim that they were the victims of the referee's mistake, for it was Prentice and not Bathgate who should have taken the penalty shot.

"The ref gave New York the game on a wrong call," said Detroit coach Sid Abel. The Rangers later agreed with Abel, but they weren't about to relinquish their opportunity to gain entrance to the play-offs. The gloating New Yorkers were soon to get their comeuppance, however, in a strange quirk of irony in the play-offs. Once again, a wrong call by the referee thwarted a team's chances for victory.

Underdogs in the semifinal round against the second-place Toronto Maple Leafs, the Rangers lost the first two games at Toronto, but then returned to the friendly confines of Madison Square Garden and stunned the visitors with 5–4 and 4–2 victories. With regained momentum the New Yorkers returned to Toronto for the pivotal fifth game of the best-of-seven series.

The game, played on April 5, 1962, at Maple Leaf Gardens, was a marvelous display of hockey. After three periods of regulation time, the evenly matched clubs were tied, 2–2. One period of sudden-death overtime failed to bring about a decision, which meant another session of pulsating sudden death. It was the Rangers who opened the attack and seemed on the verge of beating ancient Johnny Bower in the Toronto goal. But the New York shots fell short, and the Leafs regrouped and counterattacked shortly after the four-minute mark.

Gump Worsley, who had played competently throughout the series for New York, was tested on a long shot. He stopped the drive but somehow lost the puck as it fell behind him, directly in front of, but not over, the goal line. Worsley fell backward, like a man in the act of fainting, and landed on top of the puck.

Having thwarted the drive, Worsley remained horizontal awaiting the referee's whistle to signal the end of play. One second, two seconds, three seconds elapsed, and still no whistle. Nevertheless, Worsley was convinced that enough time had elapsed to compel a stoppage of play, so he lifted his head off the rather uncomfortable puck-pillow and prepared to rise for the ensuing face-off.

The face-off never came.

The referee apparently had lost track of the puck momentarily and by mistake delayed blowing his whistle. At exactly the moment that Worsley lifted his head, Toronto center Red Kelly skated across the mouth of the goal, saw the unguarded puck big as life, and quickly pushed it into the cage. The red light flashed on and the Maple Leafs won the game, 3–2.

Stunned by the setback, the Rangers lost the sixth game of the series, 7–1, and were eliminated from the playoffs. On their long trip back to New York, the defeated players were heard to echo the same remark made by the Red Wings only weeks earlier—"The blankety-blank referee made a wrong call."

Worsley, the unfortunate victim, was to be plagued by misfortune throughout his long and colorful career. As much as anyone, the Gump symbolized the beleaguered goaltender who, like Buster Keaton in the movies, fought on despite misfortune. But Worsley really was unique in his profession. He thought nothing of standing unflinchingly in front of 120-mile-an-hour shots, but he had an obsessive fear of flying. The problem began to plague Worsley when he was a nineteen-year-old playing for the New York Rovers, a minor-league farm team of the Rangers. The Rovers were flying east after a game in Milwaukee when flames began spouting from one of the engines on the plane. It was touch and go for about a half hour as the pilot sought to control the blaze and find a suitable place to land. He finally accomplished both and the aircraft touched down in Pittsburgh.

Physically, Worsley emerged from the plane unharmed. But the traumatic experience of seeing an engine enveloped in flames at twenty thousand feet is not something easily forgotten.

And Gump didn't forget.

Throughout his long and successful NHL career, he worried more about the takeoff of Boeing 707s than he did about the takeoff of those black rubber pucks that flew in his face. Somehow Worsley managed to cope with the strain until 1967, when the league expanded to twelve teams and he was compelled to fly from coast to coast as his team, the Montreal Canadiens, fulfilled their schedule. Then, in the 1968–69 season, it finally happened. Happy-go-lucky Gump Worsley cracked under the strain.

He was en route to Chicago when he leaned over to his seat companion, trainer Larry Aubut, and whispered, "Get Big John!"

"Big John" was Jean Beliveau, the team captain. He listened to Worsley and counseled, "Wait 'til we get to Chicago. Then we'll see what happens."

But the Gump had made up his mind—he was going to quit. As soon as the team landed in Chicago, he phoned his wife and the Canadiens' manager, Sam Pollock, and told them he had had it. No more flying, no more playing. Pollock patiently listened and suggested that Worsley return home. A week later Gump was working with a Montreal psychiatrist, trying to understand and cope with his fear of flying.

"We talked a lot," said Worsley. "He tried to work me through it. He helped a lot. At first, I just took it easy. My wife and I started to go to the odd game when the club was at home. Then I started skating again all alone, and finally I put on the pads. Pretty soon I felt not bad."

Worsley managed to recover enough of his aplomb to return to the Montreal lineup as the Canadiens entered the homestretch of the 1968–69 campaign. The Flying Frenchmen finished in first place in the East Division and went on to win the Stanley Cup, and Worsley played a key role in the triumph. As for the plane trips, well, he reached a degree of resignation over that problem. "I know I have to fly," Worsley said. "It's part of the game now. On charters it's not so bad. I spend my time in the cockpit. It feels different up there because the pilot explains things and you can see what's going on."

The Canadiens signed the Gump to another contract in 1969–70, for they believed that he had licked his flying phobia. And he had. But midway in the season the Gump once again left the team. This time, it was another phobia–practice phobia. Management said Worsley was out of shape. Manager Pollock suggested that Gump spend a few weeks trimming off his fat in the minors. Worsley refused and, after a clash with coach Claude Ruel, he was suspended from the team.

Later, Worsley, who had been a chief cog in the first-place Canadiens' machine a year earlier, was traded to Minnesota, a club that had gone twenty games without a win. But the moment the beleaguered Worsley arrived in Minneapolis, the North Stars regrouped, regained their equilibrium, and, with the pudgy, airsick, and out-of-shape Worsley leading the way, marched to a play-off berth. Such an ironic twist of fate suited the colorful goaltender's sense of humor perfectly.

For the net minders who happened to play for the Boston Bruins during their drought years of the fifties, goaltending was not particularly enjoyable, either. During one period of extreme bombardment of the Bruins' cage, the Boston management could have been forgiven if it had taken out a life insurance policy for every goaltender who put on a Bruin uniform.

Roger Barry, the hockey writer for the Quincy, Massachusetts, *Patriot-Ledger,* was so moved by the Beantown blitz that he wrote an article about the "discovery" of the perfect Bruin goalie. The man's name was something like Pierre Lafong and he purportedly was discovered in the wilds of northern Quebec. What made Pierre so ideal for the position, said Barry, was that he measured almost a perfect five by five—five feet tall and five feet wide— thereby blocking all but a few inches of the goal area. In order to put the puck past him, the opposition would require a derrick or a blowtorch.

Publication of the "Perfect Pierre" story in the Boston Garden hockey program caused a tidal wave of excitement around the league over this truly amazing find. Bruin fans were delirious with joy and opponents wondered with consternation just how they would cope with this Chinese Wall of a goalie.

Barry was somewhat startled by the reaction. "It was only a gag," he said. "Mr. Five-by-Five was merely a product of my imagination, not the Bruins' farm system." But the beleaguered Boston hockey fans, who were prepared to cling to any thread of hope about their team, accepted the myth of "Mr. Five-by-Five," and, at least temporarily, converted it into their own form of reality.

16. THE GOALIE WHO SCORED A GOAL

Ever since R.F. Smith drew up the first rules for hockey in the late 1800s, it has been generally accepted that a goalie's place is in that abbreviated area between the posts. In fact, just about every man who has ever laced on the forty-pound leather pads has done his goaltending in close proximity to the cage. There is, however, an exception to this and the following brief story tells of a goalie who ranged far afield with a rather spectacular result.

Chuck Rayner, who tended goal in New York—first for the old Americans and later for the Rangers—harbored an obsessive desire to spring away from his nets, dipsy-doodle through the enemy's defense, and score a goal against his opposite number on the other side of the rink.

During World War II, Rayner's fantasy was realized. Playing for an all-star Royal Canadian Army team, he was guarding the goal when a ten-man scramble developed behind his net. Suddenly the puck squirted free and slid temptingly in the direction of the other goal.

What's more, there was nobody between Rayner and the puck.

The bush-browed goalie got the message. With a five-stride head start on his pursuers, Rayner charged down the ice. His opponents were so startled by the maneuver that they just stopped in their tracks to watch. What they saw was a phenomenon: Rayner skated to within firing distance and whacked the puck into the net. A goalie had scored a goal! The feat has never been duplicated in big-league hockey.

17. THE MOST INJURED MAN IN HOCKEY

Injuries are as much a part of hockey as the ice and the puck. It is uncommon for a skater to survive a career in the NHL without suffering a few broken bones, losing his front teeth, and acquiring several dozen stitches. Late in the forties an insurance company made the mistake of offering special policies to big-league hockey players. For every stitch a player suffered, the insurance firm gave him a check for $25. By the end of the season the company realized that it would go out of business unless it immediately eliminated the policies.

Had such coverage been in effect in the fifties and sixties, Marcel Pronovost, who played for the Detroit Red Wings and Toronto Maple Leafs, would now be a very rich man. Of all modern hockey players, perhaps Pronovost has the most claim on the unofficial trophy for the most injured man in hockey. Episodes of Marcel's derring-do are legend around NHL rinks. He broke into big-league hockey with Detroit in the Stanley Cup play-offs of 1950 and was around to play a few games for the Toronto Maple Leafs in the 1969–70 season. In between, he collected hundreds of stitches and innumerable broken bones.

Once, in a game against the Chicago Black Hawks, Marcel sped across the blue line as two husky Chicago defensemen dug their skates into the ice, awaiting his arrival. They dared Pronovost to pass. "I decided there was only one move," said Marcel, "bust through the middle."

Even the most ironfisted hockey players shudder at the thought of crashing a defense, but Pronovost wasn't thinking about getting hurt. He never did. He eyed the two-foot space between the Hawks, boldly pushed the puck ahead, and leaped at the opening.

Too late. The crouched defensemen slammed the gate, hurling Pronovost headfirst over their shoulders. In that split second of imminent danger—when even the strongest of men would automatically have shut their eyes—Marcel looked down and saw the puck below him. He swiped at it, missed, and had to settle for a three-point landing on his left eyebrow, nose, and cheek.

A few minutes later the doctor was applying ice packs to Pronovost's forehead as he lay on the dressing room table. Marcel's skull looked as if it had been the loser in a bout with a bulldozer. His nose was broken and listed heavily toward starboard. His eyebrow required twenty-five stitches. "And my cheekbones," Marcel recalled in his deep tone, "felt as if they were pulverized." He was right, they were cracked like little pieces of china.

"What hurt most," says Pronovost, whose face is as craggy as an alpine peak, "was that I had to miss the next two games. As for the injuries, I didn't think twice about them." Marcel always regarded his misfortunes casually. "To me," he says, "accidents are as common as lacing on skates. One of the prizes of my collection of injuries is a break of the fourth dorsal vertebra."

Other athletes have a standing challenge from Pronovost to match their injuries against his incredible list of damages, which includes a broken jaw, seven smashed teeth, thirteen broken noses, a hernia, a damaged Adam's apple, a hemorrhaged eyeball, two broken wrists, elbow chips, a severed cheek vein, a brain concussion, and separated shoulders.

When discussing Marcel's casualties, sportswriters burned up most of their typewriter ribbons on his broken noses. They made good copy. For instance, in 1959, after Pronovost had broken his beak for the thirteenth time, he examined it with the air of a true connoisseur and said, "Frankly, I was disappointed. After a few towels were put on I could see out of both eyes. The first time I broke my nose in a hockey game, my eyes were swollen shut for three days."

The six-foot, 190-pound Pronovost discussed his wounds as proudly as a big-game hunter exhibits his catches. A while ago Marcel was talking about athletes and injuries, and when the talk got around to baseball Pronovost noted the time several years earlier that Whitey Ford had walked off the mound in the middle of the sixth game of the 1961 World Series. "You're not going to fault Whitey for leaving the game," Marcel said between sips of orange juice. "He had a broken leg, didn't he?" It was explained that Ford's injury had been nothing more than a bruised right toe.

At first Marcel didn't believe it. He spat a piece of orange rind into an ashtray. "That's the difference between a contact game like ours and a game like baseball. I'm not knockin' baseball. You can't compare the feelings a guy gets in a hockey game with those in a baseball game. But, hell, if I jaked it on account of a bruise, I'd miss more games than I play. Like one night I had a sore knee but I didn't even think twice about missing the game."

During the 1961 Stanley Cup finals, Pronovost committed what Ford would undoubtedly consider a scandalous act. He played four games on a badly cracked ankle. Marcel would arrive at the arena on crutches, play the game, and then put the foot back in a cast again. A teammate who watched him suffer through each torturous turn on the ice put it simply: "He played on guts alone, nothing else!"

Nobody forced him to do it, for Detroit carried ample substitutes. Pronovost could have chucked the game for a seat on the bench just as he could have when he was baptized as a hockey player at the age of seven. That was in his hometown of Shawinigan Falls, Quebec, where the ponds freeze in November and every kid owns a pair of skates.

"I first got hurt in a game of shinny," said Pronovost, running his finger over his scarred left eyebrow. "Ran into a high stick and wound up with a badly cut eye. I could have used a couple of stitches on that one. But with twelve kids in our family we couldn't afford a doctor."

Five years later Marcel couldn't afford to refuse a doctor. His school team had just won a big game. While his colleagues whooped it up on the ice, Marcel executed a gleeful backward pirouette. Unknown to him, one of his teammates was completing a forward pirouette. They both were on the same track. Marcel's ballet resulted in a bad cut and a broken nose.

"I fell on top of him," said Pronovost. "The back of his skate, you know, the sharp point, cut into my forehead and ripped open an area around my left eye. Missed my eyeball by about an eighth of an inch." By this time the Pronovost clan had enough money for a doctor, so Marcel was rushed to the hospital for an operation. When it was over his father suggested that Marcel might live past the age of fifteen if he followed some advice: "Quit hockey!"

"That was on a Wednesday," Marcel recalled. "They took me home from the hospital on Saturday morning and told me to rest. By Saturday afternoon I couldn't take it anymore. I sneaked out, went to the rink, started playing again. When my father found out, he gave me up as a lost cause."

Hockey coaches disagreed with Papa Pronovost. They not only believed Marcel would survive but, by God, that he would be a damn good hockey player to boot. Marcel justified their confidence by moving from his grammar school team up to the Shawinigan Tech team and finally to a contract with the Windsor Spitfires, Detroit's junior farm team.

Even at Windsor injuries trailed him like a shadow. Once, Marcel galloped after a loose puck along the boards. The blade of his stick hopped over the puck and stuck into the boards. Before Marcel could jam on the brakes, the stick shaft slipped up his leg and rammed into his groin. "That's when I got the hernia," Pronovost related. "The doctors wanted to operate at the time but I wouldn't have it. I wanted to play. So I wore a guard over the injury and a goalkeeper's jockstrap and kept on playing. Yeah, I had the operation—after the season."

Two years later he turned pro with Omaha in the United States Hockey League and won a reputation as a reckless, end-to-end rushing defenseman. He set a point record for defensemen and graduated to the Detroit Red Wings at the end of the 1949–50 season after winning the USHL rookie award.

If the kid's nerves were going to crack, now would be the time. Detroit went seven games with Toronto in the Stanley Cup semifinals before beating the Leafs in sudden-death overtime. Then they went another pulsating seven games and a double overtime final to beat the Rangers for the cup. Not yet twenty years old, Pronovost played like a cold-blooded veteran and saw his name engraved for the first time on the Stanley Cup.

When he came to training camp the fall following his rookie year, Marcel fully expected to crash the Detroit varsity. Instead, he was blasted right out of the NHL. On a patented Pronovost rush, he tried bisecting the defense of iron men Leo Reise and Bob Goldham. The three players fell to the ice and Goldham's stick creased Marcel's face. His noble charge cost Marcel a fractured cheekbone and a ticket to Indianapolis to play in the minors. But after thirty-four injury-free games there he was recalled and for years was a fixture on the Detroit defense.

"Once I got back to the NHL I began to enjoy myself," he said. "I only missed a single game in the 1951–52 season. I was going along fine the next year until a January game against the Montreal Canadiens."

Bouts between the Canadiens and the Red Wings always seemed on the brink of total warfare. Ted "Old Scarface" Lindsay, the Detroit terror, once underlined the feelings between the two rivals: "I'd play those Frenchmen for nothing, just so I could go out on the ice and tear a piece out of them." The Montrealers had similar homicidal thoughts on the subject. Even though Marcel was a Frenchman, the Canadiens had no particular love for him and they proved it.

Early in the game Pronovost stole the puck at center ice and sped toward the goal. "There was only one man with a chance to catch me," he remembered, "Maurice Richard." With a consummate hatred for any Detroiter, Richard swerved suddenly toward center to nail his man.

"Out of the corner of my eye I saw him coming," said Marcel bitterly. "But I wasn't concentrating on him as much as I was on the goal. I was about to shoot when a hunk of lumber smashed against my jaw. I was out cold." The speeding Richard, his stick brandished high, had hacked Marcel's mouth, broken his jaw, and pushed in four front teeth.

"Funny," Marcel said, "I remember skating off the ice under my own power, but I can't remember whether I finished the game or not. That night I traveled to Detroit by train. I didn't do much sleeping. I didn't eat any breakfast either. When I got home my wife said my face had swelled up so much I looked like a monkey. I guess the worst part of it was that I missed a few teeth."

Being normal in many respects, hockey players dread the grind of a dentist's drill as much as the next fellow. "The toughest, most fearless people I know are hockey players," admitted Dr. Henry H. Weishoff, the New York Rangers' dentist. "But when they sit in my chair, they're scared like everyone else. I've had players come into my office with cracked teeth and exposed nerves. They can take the pain beforehand, but when they get in that chair it's murder. Red Sullivan, the ex-Ranger center, used to go through the tortures of hell when he came in here."

Naturally, the exception was the fearless Pronovost. He'd walk into a dentist's office as calmly as he would go to the corner grocery. "I was never bothered by the dentist," said Marcel, trying not to sound like a hero. "I guess it's like anything else in life—some people are bothered and others aren't."

If anything bothered Pronovost it was missing a game, especially in March, 1954, when a collision sidelined him for nine contests, the most he has ever missed. It happened in a game against Chicago. Marcel was careening down the right side of the rink at about twenty-five miles an hour when his skate hit a rut in the ice.

"Lee Fogolin, the big Chicago defenseman, was standing there waiting to belt me," said Marcel, "but I fooled him. Unintentionally, of course." Derailed by the rut, Marcel plunged headfirst like a crazy locomotive, the top of his head crashing into boxcar Fogolin's shoulder. "He hit me so hard," Fogolin said, "I was dizzy for the rest of the night." The force of the blow broke the fourth dorsal vertebra in Pronovost's back.

"At first I had spasms and couldn't move my arms," Marcel said. "I went to the dressing room, felt better, came back, and finished the game. On the next day, I went bowling. When I got home I couldn't move. The doc said it was my back. So I had to sit out nine games."

Marcel's rib cage has been battered almost as much as his belabored nose. Marcel's old teammate, Ted Lindsay, once chased an opponent toward the waiting Pronovost. The enemy took a quick left turn and the pursuing Lindsay rammed into Marcel's chest. The impact was enough to separate a few of Marcel's ribs. Another time, Dickie Moore, the onetime Montreal villain, tried to embed Marcel in the sideboards. Moore hit him so hard that the penalty box door burst open and Pronovost fell full tilt into the open boards. More separated ribs.

A few weeks later Marcel tried the same trick. This time he bounced Marc Reaume off the boards expecting similar results, but the boards didn't cooperate. Reaume came off the boards like a tennis ball. He hit Marcel in the eye for nine stitches. Less than a week later, Marcel got too close to Jackie Leclair of Montreal, who was following through on a backhand. Marcel's poor, battered left eye was in the way again—seven stitches. "When it comes to my best cut," Marcel said analytically, "I'd have to go with the twelve-stitch job I got in Chicago. Pierre Pilote clipped me with his stick."

The white line below the crown of Marcel's dome is evidence that, prior to his recent death, goalie Terry Sawchuk had the hardest shot of any net tender in hockey. In 1953, Marcel was sprawled on the ice in front of his net. Suddenly he felt a rap on the head—as if someone had nudged him with a pile driver. Attempting to clear the puck, Sawchuk had clobbered Marcel instead of the puck and practically beheaded his roommate.

A shoulder separation, one of Marcel's most painful injuries, only proves that a clean play can be as damaging as a dirty one. Late in December, 1957, the Wings were playing in Chicago. Although Pronovost had heard about the Hawks' sharp rookie, Bobby Hull, he underestimated the young player's strength. "When he bore down on me," Marcel revealed, "I thought I'd be able to hit him straight up and stop him. He fooled me and went low." The point of Hull's elbow dug into Pronovost's chest and up his shoulder, driving the shoulder into left field. "It was a clean play," Marcel admitted with unwavering admiration. "I wish I'd have thought of that."

Considering the seriousness of his injuries, Marcel's durability has amazed writers. "The way he drops in front of shots," a Detroit writer once said, "you'd think a puck would have blasted right through his ribs and out the other side." Actually, this nearly happened in a game against Montreal. Jean Beliveau, whose shot zooms at an estimated ninety to one hundred miles per hour, nearly drove the rubber through Marcel's eye. As the Canadiens' ace cracked the blade of his stick against the puck, Marcel fell to his knees about ten feet away. The puck boomed against Pronovost's right eye, sending him to the ice.

"They turned the lights out on me that night," he said with a laugh. "But I guess I was lucky. The puck hit me flat. If it had hit me on the sharp side, I would have lost an eye. All I had was some hemorrhaging."

He was even luckier in a game at Madison Square Garden. With less than a minute to play and the Wings hanging onto a one-goal lead, a wave of blue-shirted Rangers invaded Red Wing territory. Andy Bathgate, the Ranger star, sent a cross-ice pass to teammate Dean Prentice. Knowing that if the puck reached Prentice the Wings would be in trouble, Pronovost dived in the path of the pass and intercepted it. But the momentum carried him into the wake of another speeding Ranger, whose razor-sharp blade sliced into his cheek. It severed a vein and barely missed cutting his eye.

Marcel was once asked whether he was afraid of dropping in front of shots. He said that it's not as dangerous as it looks. "Most of the time you get the puck in the ribs or the soft part of the stomach. It'll sting you, but if you fall at the right time and the right place you'll catch the puck before it gets too much power. If you don't do it right, you're in trouble."

When asked if the play made him nervous, he answered, "No more than crossing the street scares you. You don't think about getting hit by a car and I don't think about getting hurt on the ice. If I did, I'd probably go crazy. There's so many things to worry about.

"Like the time I was playing for Omaha, I once went in alone on Freckles Little, the Tulsa goalie. I fell over him when he came out to block my shot. The back of my head hit the steel goal pipe. If it was the front of the head I'd have had a fractured skull. With the back it was only a concussion. If I was to worry about it I'd never make a play like that again and I'd be useless to the team."

At that time, insurance companies were still paying hockey players for wounds suffered in combat. "I could have used the dough," he said, "but I sorta felt the insurance should be saved for something really important. I was getting stitches all the time. If I kept collecting for them, the company might have got fed up when I broke my arm or collarbone."

Not all of Marcel's scars are souvenirs of his job. Once, he stepped on a rake in front of his house. The rake handle flew up and scored a direct hit on his proboscis. Another time he was playing with his children. Marcel went to his right; his son Michel went to his left. Michel got the decision, Marcel broken nose number ten.

When Marcel was asked whether that particular broken nose had him off the ice, the question seemed to him as curious as if one had asked an astronaut whether he was afraid of heights. "My game is a contact sport," he replied. "It's a game of men. I expected to get bounced and get my lumps. I also expected to play in every single game. It's as simple as that.

"You're tougher than baseball or basketball players. A hangnail and they're out for two weeks. I won't knock them. They play a different game and maybe they react to it differently than I react to mine. But the whole point is this—if I went out on the ice and thought I wasn't going to get hurt, I just wouldn't have been a hockey player."

18. THE RIOT TO END ALL RIOTS

One of the most ironic aspects of hockey history is the fact that the NHL's most explosive goal scorer, Maurice "Rocket" Richard, never led the league in total scoring at any time in his eighteen-year career. This anomaly was caused by two factors—first, Richard was primarily a goal getter and not a playmaker, and, second, points for cheap assists were awarded to players in the forties and fifties, so it was much easier for a playmaker to earn points than it was for a goal scorer like Richard.

Nevertheless, Richard was leading the league in total points scored during the homestretch of the 1954–55 season and had a good chance to win the Art Ross Trophy for the first time in his career. What's more, his Montreal Canadiens were neck and neck with the Detroit Red Wings in the race for the league championship and appeared to have the edge, thanks to such high-scoring forwards as Bernie "Boom Boom" Geoffrion, Jean Beliveau, Dickie Moore, and Bert Olmstead.

114

In March, 1955, the Canadiens were on the threshold of becoming the greatest team in hockey history. Although they won that distinction the following season, conceivably they could have earned it in the spring of 1955 had misfortune not struck the Rocket at the most ill-timed moment in his career.

It had been a successful but stormy season for Richard. He had been assaulted by many of the league's mediocre checkers and had clashed with NHL president Clarence Campbell over a column Richard had written for a French-language newspaper. Then, during the final week of the season, there was the added pressure of staying ahead of the pack in the race for the coveted but elusive scoring title.

As a result, the brooding Rocket was in a tense state on the night of March 13, 1955, as he prepared for a game with the Bruins at Boston Garden. "My back hurts like the dickens," he told a reporter. "I feel beat." He was angry with himself for missing a goal against Toronto on the previous Thursday, and he worried about his chances of winning the scoring championship, the Stanley Cup, and the $1,000 league bonus that would go with it.

His fury increased during the game as Boston built up a 4–2 lead. But the Canadiens still had a chance. For with only six minutes remaining, the Bruins were penalized and Montreal coach Dick Irvin removed his goalie, sending six men up the ice.

As Richard swooped over the Boston blue line for a play on the goal, he felt the stick of Bruin defenseman Hal Laycoe graze the left side of his head. Referee Frank Udvari immediately signaled a penalty and whistled Laycoe off the ice. Before Laycoe could enter the penalty

115

box, Richard rubbed his head and saw a smear of blood on his hand. Impulsively, he rushed Laycoe and belabored him about the face and shoulders with his stick. Laycoe recovered from the blows, dropped his gloves and stick, and beckoned Richard to fight him barehanded.

At that point the fight probably would have simmered down if linesman Cliff Thompson had not intervened. A former Bruins' defenseman, Thompson intensified the brouhaha by grabbing Richard's stick away from him. The Rocket flew into a rage. He picked up a loose stick and hacked away at Laycoe until the stick splintered over the Bruin. Again, Thompson rushed him, and again Richard slashed at Laycoe until finally Thompson brought the Rocket to the ice.

This time a Montreal player intervened and helped the Rocket to his feet. Richard charged Thompson, smashing the official until his face was bruised and his eye blackened. By then the Rocket had vented his anger and was ushered to the first aid room.

Referee Udvari tossed Richard out of the game and levied an automatic $100 fine against him, but everyone in the hockey world knew that an additional penalty would be imposed. The question was—would Clarence Campbell penalize Richard with another fine or would he take an extreme position and suspend Richard during the final week of the season?

Campbell ordered a special hearing in his Montreal office on March 16. The Rocket was penitent as he left Montreal Western Hospital, where he had been under observation for the head wound he had suffered. He drove with coach Dick Irvin and assistant manager Ken Reardon to see Campbell at NHL headquarters in the Sun Life

Building. All Richard could say during the ride was, "I always seem to be getting into trouble."

The hearing lasted three hours. Campbell heard accounts from Boston coach Lynn Patrick, referee-in-chief Carl Voss, linesman Sammy Babcock, Udvari, Thompson, Richard, and Laycoe. Richard's defense rested on a claim that he had been stunned by the head blow and didn't comprehend what he was doing. "I don't remember what happened," Richard told Campbell. Later he added, "When I'm hit I get mad and I don't know what I do."

Campbell, both a lawyer and a former referee, seemed well suited to decide Richard's punishment. He mulled over his notes for more than an hour and then began writing his decision. "I had a hard time making up my mind," he said. At four o'clock he summoned reporters and announced his sentence: "Richard is suspended from playing in the remaining league and play-off games."

Within minutes, word of Campbell's decision was on the lips of nearly every Montrealer, all of whom reacted with bitterness and disbelief. "No sports decision ever hit the Montreal public with such impact," commented *Maclean's Magazine*. "It seemed to strike at the very heart and soul of the city."

Upon hearing the news, a bus driver fell into a daze, ignored a flashing railway crossing signal, and almost killed his passengers. The Russian delegation extended its sympathy to every Canadien guest present during a social gathering at the Soviet Embassy in Ottawa. A paranoid feeling swept the Canadien clan. One of the Rocket's former teammates expressed it best when he met Richard minutes after the decision was released. "They've been after you for years, Rocket," said Elmer Lach, "and now they've got you."

Richard couldn't believe the news. Accustomed to fines and verbal rebukes but not a suspension, the Montreal ace left for his home a confused man. "I was so disappointed," he said later, "I didn't know whether I would stay in Montreal or not. My first impulse was to go to Florida. But I changed my mind. I wanted to watch my team play. I didn't want the fans to get the idea that I was no longer interested just because I was suspended."

Meanwhile, Campbell was beginning to detect signs of the mounting wave of fury that was soon to engulf Montreal. A man phoned the NHL office and told Campbell's secretary, Phyllis King, that he was an undertaker. "Tell him," the voice said, "that he'll be needing me in a few days." Another caller warned Campbell, "I'm going to kill you. I'm no crank—but I'm going to blow your place up." Several women phoned and wept without uttering a word. Campbell was vilified with every curse available in English *and* French.

Not surprisingly the ethnic question emerged immediately. "If the Rocket's name was Richardson," wrote one French-Canadian fan, "you would have given a different verdict." Gerard Filion, editor of the Montreal daily *Le Devoir*, observed, "Had Campbell been a Frenchman he would have been killed then and there."

Some observers believe that the ensuing explosion might have been averted if the political-intellectual community had not supported Richard so ardently. Jean Drapeau, the mayor of Montreal, promptly denounced Campbell. "It would not be necessary," said Drapeau, "to give too many such decisions to kill hockey in Montreal." The editorial pages of Montreal's newspapers were nearly unanimous in the opinion that the penalty was too severe.

By the afternoon of March 17, a growing battalion of fans stalked the sidewalks around the ancient Montreal Forum, where the Canadiens were to play the Detroit Red Wings that night. Some carried signs reading *"Vivre Richard* (Long Live Richard)" and *"A bas Campbell* (Down with Campbell)."

Neither the fans nor the police nor Forum officials were certain about Campbell's plans for the game. Nobody really expected him to attend, but he had never declared that he wouldn't show up. "If he does go," warned an assistant police inspector, "there'll be trouble."

Late that afternoon Campbell declared he had no intention of missing the game. The tall, graying president, who rarely loses his cool, explained his position quietly and with apparent logic. "I'm a season ticket holder," he said, "and a regular attendant, and I have a right to go. I felt that the police could protect me. I didn't consult them and they didn't advise me not to attend."

Mayor Drapeau later challenged Campbell's version of the story. The mayor insisted that a police official had suggested that Campbell remain at home, but when Campbell insisted on going to the game, the officer urged him to drive his car and leave it in a garage two blocks east of the Forum. Unlike Campbell, Richard was hesitant about making an appearance. However, when his wife said she wanted to see the game, the Rocket felt obliged to go along with her.

The opening face-off was scheduled for 8:30 P.M., and by that time more than six hundred militant demonstrators had gathered on St. Catherine Street West, in front of the

Forum, and on Atwater and Closse Streets, which bound
the side entrances. Unobtrusively, Richard and his wife
moved through the crowd and camped in seats near the
goal judge's chair at the end of the rink. Campbell, who
had dined at the Montreal Amateur Athletic Association,
was delayed by his meal and arrived at the garage two
blocks east of the Forum later than he had anticipated.

By the time Campbell and his party arrived—he was
accompanied by his secretary, Miss King—the police had
their hands full containing the crowd that was growing
increasingly more belligerent. Campbell managed to find a
policeman and asked him to escort the party to their seats.
The constable summoned a police inspector, who accompanied the duo to the referees' room where Campbell
hung up his coat. Then they walked to Campbell's box at
the south end of the rink and took their seats to watch the
game in progress.

Detroit had already taken at 2–1 lead and the Canadiens appeared disorganized without the Rocket, so the fans
were distressed. As soon as Campbell took his seat, a
thunderous roar filled the Forum. *"Va-t'-en, va-t' en,"* the
crowd screamed (loosely translated, this means "beat it!").
The more the fans chanted, the worse the Canadiens
performed. By the end of the first period, the local heroes
were behind, 4–1, and it was obvious that Campbell was
in trouble.

As the intermission approached, a torrent of debris
poured down upon the NHL president and his guests.
Miss King's white straw hat was knocked off her head by
an overshoe. A bunch of assorted fruit defaced Campbell's
dark green hat, but most of the missiles fell wide of the
mark. To pinpoint the target for missile wielders, a fan six

seats behind Campbell rose to direct the fire of those above him.

When a soda pop bottle struck a woman nearby, several fans implored Campbell to leave, but the implacable president remained seated and even managed to smile. "I tried to avoid doing anything that would provoke the crowd," said Campbell. But the slightest movement was enough to spur an attack. A youngster swooped down from the aisle above and pretended to shake hands with Campbell. When the president reached forward, the youth hurled several punches in his face. The police eventually grabbed the young man, but just as quickly let him go.

In time, the siren wailed heralding the end of the first period. Normally Campbell would have returned to the referees' room, but this time he remained seated in order to avoid provoking the crowd any further. A minute later a man in his twenties rushed forward and squashed two tomatoes against Campbell's chest.

Soon, dozens of fans from the bleachers began charging toward Campbell's unprotected seat. Ordinarily, a police guard would have surrounded Campbell's box, but the demonstration at the barricades outside the Forum had become so threatening that all the available police inside had rushed down to guard the door. So the president remained exposed and unguarded by police.

At exactly 9:11 P.M., Campbell's party was completely encircled by a mob that observers contended was bent on killing the president. "The ill feeling," reported *Maclean's Magazine*, "was growing more intense by the second and there was nobody to help him. Looking around at the sea of hate-filled faces, Miss King had the feeling that they were closing in for the kill."

Suddenly an explosion from a tear gas bomb shook the vast arena and thick fumes curled roofward from an aisle at the lip of the ice surface. The bomb, which had landed twenty-five feet from Campbell, detonated a feeling of panic among the spectators. The cry of fire was heard in every section of the Forum, but when onlookers began choking and rubbing their eyes they realized that there were fumes but no flames.

That a full-scale disaster didn't develop can be attributed to the police and firemen, who promptly opened all exits and swiftly moved the crowd into the streets. Campbell seized Miss King and said, "Let's get out of here." They wended their way to the first aid room, where Campbell learned that Fire Commissioner Armand Pare had refused to permit the game to continue.

Campbell conferred with Montreal's general manager, Frank Selke, and then dispatched a note to Detroit general manager Jack Adams: "The game has been forfeited to Detroit. You are entitled to take your team on its way any time now. Selke agrees, as the fire department has ordered the building closed."

Officials of both teams believed that the fans had spent their venom and the worst was over. "At first," said Selke, "it seemed as if we had seen an end to this most hectic night in Forum history. Actually, it had only begun."

As the frightened spectators poured from the Forum into the fresh air outside, they were greeted by a mob of about six thousand, composed mainly of young adults and teenagers. They attacked the emerging fans, removed their own galoshes and tossed them at police. Others hurled chunks of ice at the Forum windows, and still others found bricks and concrete chips to throw at the Forum walls. "It seemed," said Selke, "as if an angry sky had suddenly fallen on the city."

Police estimated that the crowd had swollen to at least 10,000 by 11:00 P.M., when they called for reinforcements. Like soldiers in a besieged fortress, Forum employees sought cover where they could find it.

Campbell maintained his poise as he waited in the first aid room. "I was never seriously afraid of being lynched," he insisted. "As a referee I learned something about mobs. They're cowards."

By eleven thirty the noise had abated. Jim Hunter, the Forum building superintendent, and a burly constable led Campbell and Miss King to Hunter's car in the back of the Forum. They drove the president home, and as soon as he reached his apartment he phoned his father in Edmonton to assure him he was safe.

Unaware that Campbell had escaped, the fans continued to chant for his skin at the front of the building until they realized he might have eluded them. This infuriated the rioters even more, and hundreds embarked on a more destructive expedition. "Hoodlums were whooping in every direction," said Selke. "They smashed shop windows along St. Catherine Street. They pelted trams with bottles and chunks of ice, and they set bonfires in the streets while jostling with police and looting stores along the way."

By early morning, when the rioters finally dispersed, police had arrested seventy people and had traced the rioters' trail for fifteen blocks along St. Catherine Street, counting fifty stores damaged or looted. The total loss was estimated at $100,000.

When Campbell awakened the morning of March 18, he heard rumors on the radio that he had resigned. He reported to his office promptly at 8:30 A.M. to deny them. He also denounced Mayor Drapeau, who had said that the riots occurred because of "provocation caused by Campbell's presence." The president replied, "Does he think I should have yielded to the intimidation of a bunch of hoodlums?"

That afternoon Richard drove down to the Forum, where he delivered a public address in French to the press, radio, and television, pleading for law and order. "So that no further harm will be done," he said, "I would like to ask everyone to get behind the team and help the boys win from the Rangers and Detroit."

But it was too late. Although the Canadiens defeated the Rangers on March 19, they lost their final game to Detroit on the twentieth and finished in second place. Worse still, Richard's young teammate, Boom Boom Geoffrion, won the league scoring championship, with the Rocket playing second fiddle again. Without Richard, the Canadiens were eliminated in the Stanley Cup finals by the Red Wings.

But *l'affaire Richard* did have two positive results. Proceeds from the forfeited game were donated to Paul Meger, a former Montreal player who had been suffering from a serious head injury. And Clarence Campbell married Phyllis King, his secretary who survived the ordeal with him.

19. HOCKEY'S FIRST GREAT SWEEP

Until the Stanley Cup play-offs of 1952, no team in National Hockey League history had ever swept through the semifinal and final series without losing a game. But the 1951–52 model of the Detroit Red Wings was something very special and, if any team appeared capable of accomplishing the impossible, it was this Motor City sextet.

Spearheading the Detroit attack was the Production Line of Sid Abel, Gordie Howe, and Ted Lindsay. The goaltender was the late Terry Sawchuk, who was regarded as the best in the business, and his defense was anchored by Red Kelly and Leo Reise. Detroit's reserves were so accomplished that any one of them would have been regarded as good enough to make an opponent's first team.

If any foe could tame the Detroiters it was the Toronto Maple Leafs. During the regular season the Leafs enjoyed more success against the Wings than any other club did, winning four and tying four in fourteen games. "No Detroit club has ever been in better shape, physically or mentally," said Red Wing manager Jack Adams. "But the breaks will be decisive in this series."

Adams was being unduly cautious. His Red Wings blanked Toronto, 3–0, in the opening game, in which 102 penalty minutes were called. "It started like a tea party," said Al Nickleson of the *Toronto Globe and Mail*, "and blew itself into a roaring tempest of penalties."

Captain Ted "Teeder" Kennedy of the Leafs was one of the few people in the Toronto camp to voice any optimism. "Don't worry, fellows," he told his men after the first loss, "only four more games against these guys and we'll have 'em." As it developed, Kennedy was whistling in the dark, and very feebly at that.

The Leafs were carrying two goaltenders at the time, veteran Turk Broda and the younger Al Rollins. Since Rollins had lost the opening game, Toronto manager Conn Smythe decided to try Broda in the second match at Detroit. "I made a promise to Broda in December that Turk would get in a play-off game," said Smythe, "and I've never broken a promise yet."

Broda had long been regarded as the finest clutch play-off goalie in NHL history and the one man capable of thwarting the Red Wings, but he had been on the bench most of the season. Despite his inactivity, however, the thirty-four-year-old Turk turned away the Red Wings' shots during a power play in the first period and stopped the initial drive by Metro Prystai. Then Johnny Wilson arrived on the scene to push a loose rebound into the open net and the Leafs, who never found a way to get around the Wings' goalie Terry Sawchuk, lost the game, 1–0.

The Leafs' hopes were falsely buoyed by the close score and they returned to friendly Maple Leaf Gardens for the third and fourth games of the series. Broda was in the nets again, but this time the Red Wings so outclassed Toronto that twelve-year-old Barbara Broda wept in the stands as six goals poured past her beleaguered father. "LET'S FACE FACTS!" screamed a headline in the *Globe and Mail*. "TOO MUCH CLASS."

"It's Sid Abel who makes us go," said manager Jack Adams. "He's the needler out there. We're playing better hockey than the Leafs, but I still can't forget 1942, when we beat the Leafs in three straight, then lost the series."

Rollins replaced Broda in the fourth game and the Leafs fought as hard as they could. Nevertheless, the Red Wing juggernaut was just too strong and Detroit swept the game, 3–1, and the series in four straight contests. Immediately the question was put to Adams—was this the greatest Detroit hockey team of all time?

"How can you tell?" Adams replied. "They didn't have anything to beat. All they were playing was a third-place club."

Their opponents in the final round were the second-place Montreal Canadiens, armed with the potent Rocket Richard and a formidable defense. "We will have the cup by the nineteenth of April," predicted Montreal coach Dick Irvin. "Remember that, boys."

The best the Canadiens could do in the opening game at Montreal's Forum was limit the Red Wing dreadnought to three goals as Detroit triumphed, 3–1. "Three more and we go to Florida," chortled the cocky Red Wings.

Montreal obviously was powerful enough to give the Red Wings a better challenge than third-place Toronto had, and in the second game the Canadiens held Detroit to a 1–1 tie through the first period. Then Lindsay caromed the puck off defenseman Butch Bouchard's chest and into the net, which was all Detroit needed to win the game, 2–1. A night later Lindsay scored once and his line mate Howe tallied twice to give the Wings a 3–0 win in the game and a similar lead in the series.

"The Red Wings," said a Canadian reporter, "stand on the threshold of the greatest Stanley Cup sweep in the modern-day big-league game."

Crippled by injuries to three centers, the Canadiens couldn't contain the awesome Detroit attackers. Metro Prystai scored twice and Glen Skov once to lift the Wings to a 3–0 win and the Stanley Cup as well in an incredible eight-game sweep. "This club," said a jubilant Jack Adams, "is the best-balanced Red Wing team I've had in my twenty-five years in the NHL. I'll let the figures speak for themselves and let any other club in the league try to match them."

Only one man in the world seemed ready to deny that the Red Wings were the all-time greats. That was Dick Irvin, Montreal's bitter coach. "Why should I pretend something I do not feel?" said Irvin after refusing to congratulate the winners. "No Detroit executive or player congratulated us when we won last year. Let them celebrate their victory over a hollow-shell team if they wish. I don't lose easily."

But few observers paid any attention to Irvin's sour-grapes comments. The Red Wings' grand slam was accomplished over a formidable Montreal sextet and, to this day, Jack Adams' 1952 Cup-winners are regarded as one of hockey's most powerful juggernauts.

20. A CASE OF
ORGANIZED CONFUSION

Arthur Reichert, a short, wiry man, crouched forward as the Detroit Red Wings headed toward the New York Rangers' zone. It was just past the nine-minute mark in the third period on Sunday night, November 21, 1965, and the Rangers were leading 2–1 at Madison Square Garden. Reichert, who had been a goal judge for more than twenty years, was at his usual position—just behind the Plexiglas barrier at the west end of the arena directly facing the goal cage.

At the same time Emile "The Cat" Francis, the equally small general manager of the Rangers, was sitting in his seat somewhere in the side arena urging his defensemen to thwart the enemy attack.

Parker MacDonald of the Red Wings carried the puck over the center red line with Norm Ullman, his center, speeding along at his side. The two Detroiters burst through the New York defense with Ullman now in control of the puck.

As the Wings milled in front of the cage, Ullman swiped at the puck and sent it spinning toward the goal, where Floyd Smith of Detroit added another poke. The Ranger net minder, Ed Giacomin, thrust out his gloved hand and nabbed the puck. A split second later Reichert pushed his right thumb against the button and the red light illuminated above the Plexiglas, signaling a Red Wing goal.

The moment Francis saw the red light he leaped out of his seat, dashed along the aisle, and then rushed down to the goal judge's area. By this time five Rangers were milling on the ice directly in front of Reichert, protesting that the puck had never gone in. Francis bulled his way past the spectators surrounding Reichert. "I was watching that play clearly," Francis shouted, "and that puck never crossed the red line."

Reichert, who also happened to be an accomplished tennis player and a certified public accountant, stared Francis in the eye and replied, "I've got two witnesses here to prove I'm right."

"I don't give a damn about any witnesses," screamed Francis. "You're the guy who makes the decision and you just made another rotten one."

Suddenly a burly spectator who was sitting near Reichert yelled at the Ranger manager, "Bug off, Francis, that puck was in."

Francis turned to the fan, whereupon another spectator joined the anti-Francis brigade. "One of them," the 150-pound Francis later remembered, "weighed at least 250 pounds."

A flurry of punches spread among the gaggle of fans who surrounded Francis. "Someone, I don't know who, threw the first punch," said Francis, "and things just went from there."

Three spectators jumped him and the four men rolled in the aisle directly in front of the protective glass barrier. One fan ripped Francis's jacket off his back while the second crawled on top of the Rangers' boss, tossing lefts and rights.

Vic Hadfield, the big, blond Ranger left wing, was looking directly at Francis as the manager went under. Hadfield dropped his gloves and stick, dug his fingers into the small opening between the glass panes, and lifted his skate blades onto the wooden boards. Straining, he pulled himself over the top of the barrier and fell on top of a spectator's seat on the other side. After recovering his balance, Hadfield leaped on the fans who had smothered Francis. "I saw one guy had Francis by the throat," said Hadfield.

One of the spectators pulled away from Francis and fled down the aisle. Meanwhile, Hadfield was followed over the Plexiglas barrier by Arnie Brown, Mike McMahon, Reg Fleming, and Earl Ingarfield of the Rangers. "By this time," said Francis, "the players were all around me. They caught up with the first fan, and then they bagged the second."

A total of ten Rangers scaled the tall glass barrier, but they were too late to prevent damage to their boss. Francis was cut over the left eye and left cheekbone, requiring stitches.

Reichert had sidestepped the brawling by moving to an adjacent aisle while the fuss brewed. Garden police moved in to restore order and nobody, not Francis nor any of the fans, pressed charges. "I don't want to press charges," said Francis. "I just want that goal back."

The Rangers did manage to score another goal, but Detroit tied the game less than two minutes from the finish and the contest ended in a 3–3 tie, which just served to intensify the bitterness already surrounding the tumultuous scene. Francis and Ranger president William Jennings stormed into the press room and blasted Reichert.

"I had a perfect view of the shot and the puck did not get past Giacomin," Francis insisted. "The light didn't go on immediately, and no one seemed to know who had scored—if you could call it a score. Why, none of the Red Wings even lifted their sticks to signal a goal."

Livid over the fact that referee Art Skov had upheld Reichert's decision, Jennings went a step further and said he would attempt to ban the goal judge from handling Ranger games. "I'm backing up Francis completely," said Jennings. "I am not speaking in haste when I say that Reichert is no longer welcome in Madison Square Garden and there are ways of keeping him out. There are just too many antediluvian minor officials in this league and the Rangers have to do something about it."

Jennings, a National Hockey League governor and one of the most important men in the big-league hierarchy, made his most forceful statement after the game. "The goal judges are employed by the league," Jennings went on, "but he [Reichert] won't get into this building again. Clarence Campbell, the league president, will have to come down from Montreal to get him in."

Needless to say, Ranger goalie Ed Giacomin supported his employer. And naturally Detroit Red Wing coach Sid

Abel claimed the puck had gone in. "Certainly," said Abel. "The red light was on, wasn't it?"

"Reichert could have gotten eighteen witnesses by going over to the Red Wings' bench," said Francis.

A few days later, tempers had cooled. NHL president Clarence Campbell supported Reichert and insisted that he would continue judging at Garden games. Overruled by Campbell, Jennings had no choice but to permit Reichert in the building. Francis also complied, and soon all that was remembered was the sight of ten Rangers assaulting the glass barrier.

"It was," concluded Francis in a capsule summation of the scene, "a case of organized confusion."

21. THE DEFENSEMAN
   WITH CHUTZPAH

There have been comebacks and there have been come-backs in sports, but few have ever been laced with the flair produced by defenseman Larry Zeidel in the summer of 1967. Zeidel was one of the few Jewish players in profes-sional hockey, and in Yiddish there's a word for what he did—it's called *chutzpah*. Translated, it means an inordi-nate amount of nerve, and nerve is what Zeidel had.

A rugged type, Zeidel had played briefly in the NHL for Detroit and Chicago before being demoted to the minors in 1954. He bounced around such cities as Edmonton, Hershey, Seattle, and Cleveland and seemed destined to finish his long career in the bush leagues, until in 1967 the National Hockey League expanded from six to twelve teams. Even then, nobody thought Larry had a chance to crack the NHL because he was now thirty-nine years old and completely forgotten by big-league moguls. So when the NHL managers convened in Montreal in June, 1967, to find 120 additional men to stock the six new expansion clubs, nobody was surprised that Larry Zeidel hadn't become a Minnesota North Star, a Los Angeles King, or a Pittsburgh Penguin. In fact, the *least* surprised man in the world was Larry Zeidel because he had *chutzpah*.

"I looked at those draft picks," says Zeidel, whose scarred face suggests an overhead view of a railroad freight yard. "I had to laugh. I knew I was better than half the guys they were pickin'. Then I thought about some of the fellows in the NHL. I thought of Jean Ratelle. He was a first-rate center with the Rangers. I played against Ratty three years ago when he was with Baltimore. I could handle him then, so why couldn't I handle him now?"

Although Larry Zeidel wouldn't admit it, twelve NHL managers had the answer: "You're too old." But people with *chutzpah* don't listen—they act.

One thing bugged him—he wasn't absolutely certain that his body could take seven months of NHL hockey. So he made an appointment with a doctor at the Western Reserve University medical center in Cleveland for a checkup. "I told him I got great blood lines," Zeidel said. "My father was skating after he was fifty. My mother still washes bed sheets in the bathtub. You gotta have good blood for that."

The doctor listened carefully and then tested him with an electrocardiograph machine (which records the sound of a person's heartbeat and prints a pattern of it on a long strip of paper). When he got through he told Larry Zeidel, who was thirty-nine years old, that he had the heart of a twenty-year-old. But that wasn't enough. Zeidel demanded that the doctor put it in writing because big things

135

were about to happen. Hockey was just about to be confronted with its first case of Madison Avenue hard sell.

"In order to sell myself, I needed a third-party testimonial," said Larry. "I needed something to shut up the people who'd say, 'He's too old, he's too old.' When I got the letter from the doctor, I knew I was in business."

Zeidel had always had class. When he was earning $7,000 a year with the Hershey Bears, he drove around in a new Lincoln Continental convertible. If he was going to sell himself, he'd do it right. He read an article in *Fortune* magazine about job hunting. "The key," he explained, "is getting a résumé. I went to a couple of pros. They said you gotta go first class. We had pictures taken, just like Hollywood, and then made up the brochure."

Apart from the eight-by-ten-inch glossy photos and the report from the doctor, the brochure had ten pages. The cover, in black and white, read "Résumé" in italic capital letters and then, in smaller type, "With References and Testimonials," and again in big type, "Larry Zeidel," and finally, in very small type, "Professional Hockey Player * Sales Promotion * Public Relations Executive." Underneath on the left was a picture of Larry in a hockey uniform and on the right was a picture of him wearing a Brooks Brothers suit, sitting behind a desk holding a phone.

The contents were appropriately unbashful. Page two opened with a quotation from Bud Poile, who wrote while he was manager of the San Francisco Seals: " . . . Larry is a smart hockey man and would make a fine coach." Page ten concluded with a letter from Guild, Bascom and Bonfigli, a Seattle advertising agency, thanking him for the way one of the agency's beer ads looked in the *Western*

Hockey World. Larry had once been a salesman for the magazine.

"Two things bugged me when it [the résumé] was finished," he remembered. "I was afraid they'd only think about me for the front office. I wanted to play. And I wasn't sure who to send it to. Like I didn't want to offend the club owners, but I didn't want the managers to think I was goin' over their heads."

In August, 1967, he mailed the presentation to everybody important on each of the twelve teams. Pretty soon the replies began to drift in. "I certainly am quite impressed with the material you sent me," wrote Bruce A. Norris, president of the Detroit Red Wings. "I know you always played well for us and against us. I think with your approach that you should have a fine business career. If anything develops of mutual interest, I certainly will contact you." He didn't.

Writing on behalf of Emile Francis, general manager of the Rangers, the Rangers' secretary said thanks but no thanks, adding that the Rangers were building a young defense. To add insult to injury, the secretary misspelled Larry's last name. Sammy Pollack of the Canadiens also said no. The Los Angeles Kings replied that they had no openings in sales, promotion, or public relations. The Chicago Black Hawks, Toronto Maple Leafs, Pittsburgh Penguins, Minnesota North Stars, and the St. Louis Blues never answered. There were two nibbles, however.

Frank J. Selke, Jr., now manager of the Oakland Seals, said he would discuss the matter with his coach, Bert Olmstead. William R. Putnam, president of the Philadelphia Flyers, told Larry to keep in touch. "I agree with your feeling," wrote Putnam, "that age itself does not limit a player—it is his mental attitude." Three weeks later, Selke wrote that there was no opening in his organization. There was no further response from Putnam.

But Larry Zeidel's résumé— with references and testimonials—was making the rounds in the offices of the Philadelphia Flyers. In time it landed on the desk of Keith Allen, the Flyers' coach. "The brochure," said Allen, "put the spark in our particular minds. He had played for me in Seattle so I knew a little about him. He's the same type of individual as Gordie Howe; he's got the enthusiasm of a kid."

Allen talked to Bud Poile, his boss, about Larry. But even though Larry had done some quiet scouting among American League prospects for Poile prior to the draft, Poile, one of the shrewdest men in hockey, wasn't about to do Zeidel any favors. For one thing, the Flyers had bought the entire Quebec Aces of the American Hockey League and were overloaded with defensemen. Also, they had just made some excellent draft choices—Ed Van Impe and John Miszuk from Chicago, Joe Watson and Dick Cherry from Boston, and Jean Gauthier from Montreal. And, more important, it happened to be September.

"Larry's timing was bad," said Poile. "He should have sent the brochure out in October when everybody's sorry about their choices. In September the managers all think they're going to win the Stanley Cup."

By the first of October, Poile began to see signs that indicated he might not have a cup winner. Dick Cherry had quit hockey to become a teacher. Joe Watson and Ed Van Impe were holdouts and refused to report to camp, and season ticket sales were dragging at the new Spectrum Arena in Philadelphia.

By this time Larry Zeidel considered his $200 investment an artistic success but a practical flop. He was ready to sign for another season with the Cleveland Barons when Poile showed a flicker of interest in obtaining him. "But," said Poile, "I can't do business with Bright [Paul Bright, owner of the Barons]."

Zeidel, who was then selling season tickets for the Barons, phoned Bright and told him that he ought to make some money on him (Zeidel) while there was still time. Bright agreed, but unfortunately Poile and Bright couldn't agree on anything. The deal appeared dead.

"Marie, my wife, told me there was only one thing to do, get the two of them on the phone together," said Larry. This could be done by making what the telephone company calls a *conference call*. Three parties talk on different phones at once. But after Larry dialed, nobody wanted to talk.

"Here I am payin' for the call and all I get is complete silence. So I say, 'Fellas, what's it gonna be?' Then they all start arguing. Finally, Poile said he'll give me a five-game trial and Bright asks me if I'll take it, and I say, 'Sure, I'll take my chances,' and we made the deal."

The dice were loaded, though. Poile insisted that Zeidel sign a letter giving him the right to drop Larry at will, for by this time things were looking up for the Flyers. Van Impe and Watson had finally signed their contracts, Miszuk and Gauthier were going good, and the younger John Hanna and Noel Price, both with extensive NHL experience, were now with the team. So the Flyers planned to keep Zeidel for a month, get some Jewish fans, and then let him sell tickets. To Poile it made sense— nobody would get hurt.

But coach Keith Allen wasn't concerned with the motives of the deal. Right away he started Zeidel with Joe Watson and right away the Flyers started winning and climbed to first place in the Western Division.

On November 4, the Flyers were scheduled to meet tougher competition than they had met in their division— the Montreal Canadiens. That afternoon Bernie Parent, the young goalie, and Larry Zeidel were in their room at the Queen Elizabeth Hotel in Montreal. Parent had the shakes. His questions to Zeidel showed how scared he was: "How many shots do you think they'll take at me?" "Do you really like hockey?" "We don't have a chance, do we?"

Larry Zeidel, who reads books like *Psychocybernetics: A New Way to Get More Living Out of Life,* by Dr. Maxwell Maltz, made a big impression on the young Bernie Parent. "You gotta think positive—think positive," he kept repeating. He pulled out a poem, "I Can," and read it to Parent. He fed the kid everything he had. "You gotta have a goal—a singleness of purpose."

"Yeah," Parent replied, "but they've got Beliveau and Richard and Backstrom."

"Forget it. They'll shoot from way out. Think positive, let the old subconscious come through for you."

Five hours later, the game was over, Philadelphia 4, Montreal 1. Bernie Parent had thought "positive." A week later Philadelphia went to Boston and defeated the Bruins. A week after that Philadelphia defeated the Rangers. Larry Zeidel started every game with Joe Watson at his side. Bud Poile was very disappointed, though, for Zeidel's success was keeping younger players off the ice. "It hurts
140

me because I have to keep John Hanna in civvies," he said.

In spite of Poile's disappointment, Zeidel helped lead the Flyers to the Western Division championship and the Clarence Campbell Bowl. Unfortunately, unlike the Flyers' successful windup to their 1967–68 season, Larry's saga did not have a particularly happy ending. He showed up at training camp the following fall and discovered that manager Poile had imported a couple of new defensemen. Unperturbed, Zeidel continued to drive as hard as he ever had, but this time, it appeared that the Flyers were determined to keep him on the sidelines.

About a month after the season began, Poile asked Zeidel to report to the Flyers' farm team in Quebec City. A proud man, Larry Zeidel refused. "I believed I was good enough to stay in the NHL and my record proved it," he said.

Neither side would budge, so Zeidel spent the remainder of the 1968–69 season on the sidelines. By no coincidence, the Flyers faltered badly and failed to defend their championship successfully.

The player with *chutzpah* retired from hockey in 1969 and went into the investment counseling business. Ironically, Bud Poile, the man who halted Zeidel's incredible comeback in midstream, was fired that same year.

EPILOGUE

GIVE ME HOCKEY—I'LL TAKE HOCKEY— ANY TIME

by John Kieran

I'm a fairly peaceful man and a long-time baseball fan,
Always eager when the umpire cries: "Play ball!"
And I jump with joy or terror at each hit and slide
and error
Till some game-deciding tally ends it all.
But the diamond sport is quiet to that reeling rousing riot,
To a splashing game of hockey at its prime;
It's a shindig wild and gay, it's a battle served frappé,
Give me hockey—I'll take hockey—any time.

Once, while crazy with the heat, I coughed up to
buy a seat,
Just to watch a pair of boxers grab a purse.
It was clinch and stall and shove, and "Please excuse
my glove;"

What I thought of them I couldn't put in verse.
But for fighting fast and free, grab your hat and come
with me;
Sure, the thing that they call boxing is a crime;
And for ground and lofty smacking and enthusiastic
whacking,
Give me hockey—I'll take hockey—any time.

I've an ever-ready ear for a roaring football cheer,
And I love to see a halfback tackled low;
It's a really gorgeous sight when the boys begin to fight
With a touchdown only half a yard to go.
But take all the most exciting parts of football, baseball,
fighting,
And then mix them up to make a game sublime;
It's the hottest thing on ice; you don't have to ask
me twice;
Give me hockey—I'll take hockey—any time.

Yes, for speed and pep and action, there is only
one attraction,
You'll see knockouts there a dozen for a dime,
When the bright steel blades are ringing and the hockey
sticks are swinging,
Give me hockey—I'll take hockey—any time.

ABOUT THE AUTHOR:

Stan Fischler is a well-known hockey authority and the author of a number of books on the subject, including *Gordie Howe, Goal: My Life on Ice,* and *Stan Mikita,* a Canadian best seller. His weekly column, "Inside Hockey," is carried by the Toronto star Syndicate and another, "Hockey Speakout," appears regularly in *The Sporting News.*

4879. MY GREATEST DAY IN BASEBALL 75¢

John P. Carmichael and other noted sports writers. This is a sports book that's different. Here a reader can find out how the player himself felt about his own *Greatest Day in Baseball*. And what days they were! Koufax pitching his fourth no-hitter . . . Yastrzemski's hitting rampage in the last game of the 1967 season . . . Ruth's historic home run in the 1932 World Series . . . all are here, and many more. Thirty-six great stories told by and about today's top stars and the all-time greats of baseball history. A book that will be read over and over and over again.

4877. DAREDEVILS OF THE SPEEDWAY 75¢

Ross Olney. The roar of the mighty engines . . . the smell of burning fuel . . . the constant tension . . . the high speeds . . . and the checkered flag—that is the breakneck daredevil game of auto racing. This history of the Indianapolis "500" contains true life-and-death stories of its most famous drivers.

5337. WILLIE MAYS 75¢

Arnold Hano. (revised edition) Starting from afternoon ball-catching sessions with his father—at age 3—right through the past season when he hit his 600th home run, this book is the complete story of Willie. It dramatically tells the ups and downs of his career as he rose to the top of his trade in the professional leagues.

4897. THE JOHNNY UNITAS STORY 75¢

Johnny Unitas and Ed Fitzgerald. The amazing personal account of how a hard luck kid who wouldn't quit became a star quarterback and the most phenomenal passer in pro football history. Telling about his colorful, exciting life in football, the passing wizard of the Baltimore Colts blends his personal story with his own keen analysis of football strategy and execution.

5392. RUN TO DAYLIGHT! 95¢

Vince Lombardi. The thrilling, behind-the-scenes drama of pro football, told by the greatest coach in the history of the game. Only Vince Lombardi, the fiery, dynamic leader of the champion Green Bay Packers —knows what it's really like to guide a team of world champions through the grueling schedule of a professional football season.

5393. THE MAKING OF A PRO QUARTERBACK 75¢

Ed Richter. Here is probably the most authentic book ever written on professional football. From training camp to championship game, it tells how quarterbacks learn their trade and play the game.
". . . much useful information."—The New York Times

5340. THE AMAZING METS 75¢

Jerry Mitchell. (revised edition) Jerry Mitchell, sportswriter for the *New York Post*, and cartoonist, Willard Mullin, combine their talents to tell the truth-is-funnier-than fiction story of baseball's Cinderella team. The record breaking 21-game losing streak. . . the 23-inning loss to the San Francisco Giants . . . the 1969 World Series . . . here is the whole, wacky, wonderful story of the New York Mets and their cheering, ever-faithful fans.

5316. SUPERJOE: THE JOE NAMATH STORY 95¢

Larry Bortstein. The thrilling inside story of the man who won the World's Championship for the AFL and the New York Jets, the biggest upset in pro football history—plus an eight-page photo insert.

5391. PRO FOOTBALL'S HALL OF FAME 95¢

Arthur Daley. Pulitzer Prize winning sports writer Arthur Daley of *The New York Times* has chronicled the exciting story of professional football in the profiles of the superstars and personalities who first made it great—the seventeen men selected as the first entrants of the new professional football Hall of Fame.

5330. YAZ 75¢

Carl Yastrzemski with Al Hirshberg. Triple Crown winner, Most Valuable Player of the American League for 1967, Yaz is a crowd-pleaser, a home-run hitting, hard-playing champion. He has the magnetism distinctive to all of baseball's greats, and it's that same magnetism that makes this book an exciting saga of a man who may well become a legend.

5317. GORDIE HOWE 75¢

Stan Fischler. The amazing, inspiring career story of "Mr. Hockey"—Gordie Howe—ice hockey's greatest scorer and most honored player. Gordie Howe's amazing career has spanned 21 years of rugged and inspired play in the world's fastest as well as fastest-growing sport.

5310. WINNERS NEVER QUIT 75¢

Phil Pepe. This is a collection of dramatic true stories about famous athletes who overcame adversity to become great champions. Included are the inspiring, "profiles in courage" of Mickey Mantle, Johnny Unitas, Jackie Robinson, Sandy Koufax, Rocky Marciano, and many more.

5360. MR. CLUTCH: THE JERRY WEST STORY 95¢

Jerry West with Bill Libby. Jerry West is the undisputed hero of pro basketball. A winner even in defeat, West scored a record 556 points in 18 games during the 1968-69 NBA playoffs and won the coveted title of Most Valuable Player for the series. The "hillbilly kid" from West Virginia is a veteran of ten years in the professional ranks, commanding a $100,000 contract which he fulfills through last-minute heroics that have brought him the nickname "Mr. Clutch."

5363. WILT CHAMBERLAIN 75¢

George Sullivan. Seven feet and one-sixteenth-of-an-inch tall, Wilt Chamberlain is basketball's highest scorer in history and the holder of most professional records. This biography which covers Chamberlain's career right through the 1970 season is both a fast-moving story of unprecedented achievements on the basketball court and a warm personal story of a complex human being—a thoughtful, sensitive young man trying to live a normal life in the glare of public scrutiny.

5351. STAND TALL: The Lew Alcindor Story 95¢

Phil Pepe. A basketball celebrity since his days in Power Memorial Academy, Lew Alcindor has now attained national fame as Rookie-of-the-Year for the Milwaukee Bucks. In this new biography, a long time friend tells the whole Alcindor story and analyzes the phenomenal talent that has moved the seven foot star into the sports headlines.

5352. LEN DAWSON, SUPER BOWL QUARTERBACK 95¢

Larry Bortstein. The hero of last year's Super Bowl, Len Dawson, quarterback of the World Champion Kansas City Chiefs, tells his life story—what it took to get where he is and what he hopes for in the future. Thrill-packed biography, as fast-moving as Dawson himself.

ADVENTURE

5325. FIRST ON THE MOON 75¢
Hugh Walters. The U.S. rocket Columbus and the Russian rocket Lenin are hurtling toward the moon, each carrying a human passenger intent on making the first landing on its surface.

4871. Rod Serling's TWILIGHT ZONE REVISITED 60¢
Edited by Walter Gibson. By the Emmy Award-winning TV writer, a collection of chilling stories.
Readers will share the terror of a young army officer cursed with the ability to see the glow of death on the faces of men about to die; they will fight under Custer in the battle of the Little Big Horn and marvel at those who miraculously survived—or did they?

5354. MINDS UNLEASHED 95¢
Edited by Groff Conklin. The power and the possibilities of the human mind—as uncharted as deep space—are explored in this collection of science fiction stories by masters of imagination, Isaac Asimov, Robert Heinlein, Arthur C. Clarke, Murray Leinster, Poul Anderson and others expand the limits of the mind and suggest some of the dramatic potentialities of the future.

5356. PLANETS FOR SALE 75¢
A. E. Van Vogt and E. Mayne Hull. In this future world, space travel is a commonplace and business tycoons scramble for advantage on far-flung planets. The action is in the Ridge Stars, a pioneer galaxy as yet uncontrolled by anyone, and the attempts of billionaire Arthur Blord to seize control

5313. GREAT STORIES OF SPACE TRAVEL 60¢
Groff Conklin. Who knows what strange things will confront those brave Earthlings in the years to come who dare to invade the far reaches of outer space . . . and beyond?
In these stories, a group of science fiction's greatest writers (Isaac Asimov, Ray Bradbury, A. E. Van Vogt, and others) speculate on the nature those dangers.

5306. ATTACK FROM ATLANTIS 75¢
Lester del Rey. Here is a suspense-filled tale of underwater adventure written by one of America's most honored science fiction writers. In this intriguing tale, Lester del Rey writes of an outcast race that has migrated into the sea and of a young boy who tries to escape from "the city of no return."

5344. VOYAGERS IN TIME 95¢
Edited by Robert Silverberg. A collection of twelve science fiction stories about time travel by such authors as H. G. Wells, Lester del Rey, Poul Anderson and others. Exciting, challenging accounts of voyages back and forward in time—their complexities and hazardous consequences.

4709. MYSTERY OF SATELLITE 7 50¢
Charles Coombs. When Argus 7 mysteriously explodes at an altitude of 42 miles, talk of sabotage runs loud. And suddenly three young people are catapulted from their role of privileged observers to land square in the center of the satellite mystery.

5359. THE WEAPON MAKERS 75¢
A. E. Van Vogt. One of the all-time great science fiction novels by one of the great masters. A psychological suspense novel about a man whose secret is that he is immortal and whose goal is to save the world when the weapon makers forget that they are sworn to preserve peace and attempt to take over the entire universe.

PRACTICAL

5331. 101 SUMMER JOBS 75¢
Roberta Ashley. This book gives teenagers practical ways to turn idle hours into extra dollars. Miss Ashley covers every area of summer job hunting; how to determine what kind of job each youngster is suited for, how to apply for it, and in general, how to use your skills to your best advantage. If some kids would like to try owning a small summer business, there is also a section dealing with the problems of private enterprise.

4893. SUCCESS TIPS FROM YOUNG CELEBRITIES 75¢
Dena Reed. Today's top movie, recording and TV stars offer advice to teen-agers on how to live richer, more rewarding lives. They speak candidly about the problems they personally faced and what they learned as they grew and matured.

5355. HELEN HELP US 75¢
Helen Bottell. A collection of letters called from the "Helen Help Us" column which appears in 102 newspapers nationally. Dealing with the mating game problems of young people—about going steady, falling in love, coping with early marriage and other problems, it has Helen's sound, "with-it" advice.

4809. HOW TO DEAL WITH PARENTS AND
OTHER PROBLEMS 60¢
Dr. Ernest G. Osborne. Many youngsters feel that parents and other adults don't understand them, are too strict, and are trying to run their lives. It contains guidance for you on many specific problems—bigotry in the family, the curfew battle, steady dating, the reluctance of some parents to provide sex education, and many, many more.

4872. TAFFY'S TIPS TO TEENS 75¢
Dolly Martin. A well-known newspaper-syndicated authority discusses what matters most to girls—from boys and beauty to fashion and figure care. Plus a self-improvement chart, and scores of show-how illustrations.

4887. THE BOOK OF DATING 75¢
Judith Unger Scott. Here is a book that talks to boys and girls, speaking from both sides of the dating question and revealing surprising insights about both sexes and how each thinks, plans and reacts.

5309. EINSTEIN'S HANDBOOK TO
COLLEGE ADMISSIONS $1.45
Bernice W. Einstein. Practical, up-to-date information on how to choose a college and then how to get into the college of your choice. Entrance examinations, financial aid possibilities, other specific information for the college-bound. An invaluable guide for students and parents. Completely revised and up-dated.

5323. HANDWRITING ANALYSIS FOR TEENS 75¢
Dorothy Sara. A recognized expert in the field of handwriting analysis, Dorothy Sara has written two books and many magazine articles on the subject. Here, especially for teenagers, she explains the various techniques of writing and the character traits they symbolize.

4878. TEEN LOVE, TEEN MARRIAGE 75¢
Public Affairs Committee. Edited by Jules Saltman, authors include Paul H. Landis, Professor of Sociology at Washington State University and author of a number of books for younger people, and Lester A. Kirkendall, Professor of Family Life at Oregon State University and an outstanding leader in the field. Teenagers and parents will find its eye-opening facts and wise conclusions regarding the problems of dating, sex and marriage, indispensable as a practical, everyday guide to intelligent living.

CLASSICS

4867. THE JUNGLE BOOK   50¢
Rudyard Kipling. Saved from the snatching jaws of Shere Khan, Mowgli is raised by Mother Wolf as one of her own cubs. The full original text.

5322. PENROD   75¢
Booth Tarkington. This is the only inexpensive edition of the classic which has delighted and inspired mischief-lovers for years. The story of Penrod Schofield is the story of all high-spirited American boys. Stirring up fun for himself and his friends, and trouble for his enemies and elders, Penrod does all the things that boys have always done, but somehow they turn out funnier.

4755. DADDY-LONG-LEGS   60¢
Jean Webster. A girl grows to young womanhood in an orphanage, and is sent to college by an unknown benefactor. This gay, tender, whimsical record of Judy's correspondence with her mysterious guardian has enchanted readers of all ages since it was first published. It has been translated into eighteen languages, and filmed twice, most recently with Leslie Caron and Fred Astaire playing the leading roles.

5341. DEAR ENEMY   75¢
Jean Webster. This sequel to *Daddy-Long-Legs* follows in the same engaging tradition of delightful romance. It's all here, the timeless appeal, humor and youthful wisdom that endeared Jean Webster's first youngster to millions of readers and to her now famous Daddy-Long-Legs.

4761. A LANTERN IN HER HAND   60¢
Bess Streeter Aldrich. Abbie Deal, brought up in a log cabin in Iowa, took the covered wagon trail to Nebraska as a young bride. In a rude shelter on the prairie she raised her family and stood beside her husband through all the heartbreaking struggles of the pioneer days—and became part of an epic.

5304. ANNE OF GREEN GABLES   75¢
Lucy M. Montgomery. The only unabridged reprint available. Redheaded, dreamy Anne, the orphan who brings happiness and love into the lives of her foster parents, is one of the most beloved heroines in all literature. Millions of girls throughout the world have taken her to their hearts.

4795. PETER PAN   60¢
James M. Barrie. The only inexpensive paperback version of this delightful fantasy—the classic story of Peter and Wendy and the amazing adventures that befall them in Never-Never-Land.

4763. REBECCA OF SUNNYBROOK FARM   75¢
Kate Douglas Wiggin. Living with her maiden aunts would doubtless be "the making of Rebecca" everybody thought, so the little girl with the enormous eyes and most remarkable talent for mischief was shipped to a house where children were supposed to be seen and not heard. Yet nothing could dampen Rebecca's lively spirits, and nobody could resist her winsome charm.

4841. WIND IN THE WILLOWS   60¢
Kenneth Grahame. If a poll were taken of the book best loved by boys and girls over the generations, the winner hands down, would most likely be this one. This enchanting book, packed with the adventures of Mole, Rat, Toad and their friends, is the kind of story that keeps children spellbound. Illustrated.